Pair Programming Illuminated

Pair Programming Illuminated

Laurie Williams

Robert Kessler

✦ Addison-Wesley

Boston • San Francisco • New York • Toronto • Montreal
London • Munich • Paris • Madrid
Capetown • Sydney • Tokyo • Singapore • Mexico City

The publisher offers discounts on this book when ordered in quantity for bulk purchases and special sales. For more information, please contact:

U.S. Corporate and Government Sales
(800) 382-3419
corpsales@pearsontechgroup.com

For sales outside of the U.S., please contact:

International Sales
(317) 581-3793
international@pearsontechgroup.com

Visit Addison-Wesley on the Web: www.awprofessional.com

Library of Congress Cataloging-in-Publication Data
Williams, Laurie.
    Pair programming illuminated / Laurie Williams, Robert Kessler.
        p. cm.
    Includes bibliographical references and index.
    ISBN 0-201-74576-3 (alk. paper)
        1. Computer software—Development. 2. eXtreme programming. I. Kessler, Robert R.
    II. Title

QA76.76.D47 W534 2002
005.1'1—dc21   2002066509

ISBN 0-201-74576-3
Text printed on recycled paper
1 2 3 4 5 6 7 8 9 10—CRS—0605040302
First printing, July 2002

From Laurie to Danny, Christopher, Kimberly, and Brian
Your love is the greatest gift of all.

From Bob to Julie, Alex, and Chelsea

Contents

Chapter 3: The Seven Synergistic Behaviors of Pair Programming
21

Chapter 4: Overcoming Management Resistance to Pair Programming
33

Chapter 5: Gaining Support and Acceptance from Your Peers
45

Chapter 9: Pair Rotation: Communication, Knowledge Management, and Training 73

Chapter 10: Other Issues to Consider 83

Chapter 11: Tips 'n Tricks 89

Part 3: Pair Programming Partner Picking Principles

Chapter 12: Expert-Expert Pairing 97

Chapter 13: Expert-Average Pairing 105

Chapter 14: Expert-Novice Pairing   111

Chapter 15: Novice-Novice Pairing   117

Chapter 16: Extrovert-Extrovert Pairing   123

Chapter 17: Extrovert-Introvert Pairing   129

Chapter 18: Introvert-Introvert Pairing 133

Chapter 19: Gender Nonissue 139

Chapter 20: Culture Nonissue 145

Chapter 21: The Professional Driver Problem 153

Chapter 22: "My Partner Is a Total Loser" and Other Excess Ego Problems 159

Chapter 23: "My Partner Is SO Smart" and Other Too Little Ego Problems   163

Part 4: Case Studies of Pair Programming in a Software Process

Chapter 24: Pair Programming in a Software Process Case Study: Extreme Programming (XP)   171

Chapter 25: Pair Programming in a Software Process Case Study: Collaborative Software Process (CSP)   181

Part 5: In Closing

Chapter 26: Moving Ahead, Going Beyond   195

Chapter 27: Seven Habits of Effective Pair Programmers   203

Appendix A: Pair Programming Tutorial   211

Appendix B: An Economic Analysis of Pair Programming   221

Preface

This purpose of this book is to provide you with lots of information on pair programming. If you are already pairing, then the book will give you additional insights and techniques to make your pairing even more successful. We answer many of the questions and concerns that you may have about using the technique.

In Part One, our aim is for you to gain greater understanding about pair programming. We'll describe the technique and will be looking at pair programming from many perspectives—from those of you who want to try and those who would rather not try, from those of you who are employees trying to convince their managers to let them try and those who are managers who are trying to convince their employees to try.

In Part Two, we deal with some operational details of pairing—such as furniture and hints and tips for daily operation. We discuss the importance of pair rotation and how that can lead to better knowledge management.

In Part Three, we explain benefits and shortcomings of many different kinds of pairs and the context in which each kind of pair works best. We offer ideas to help enhance the pairing and solutions for most problem pairings. Unfortunately, not all pairs will work, and we provide ways to recognize the potential problems before they happen.

Part Four gives two case studies of pair programming in different methodologies. The first describes pairing in Extreme Programming (XP), while the second discusses the Collaborative Software Process (CSP). In both cases, pair programming is an essential ingredient to success.

We conclude in Part Five with suggestions for future directions, and we enumerate Seven Habits of Effective Pair Programmers.

Who Should Read This Book

We've written this book for software development team members and their managers. When we use the term "software development team," it goes beyond those who write production code. For example, this book is certainly appropriate for team leaders and coaches, GUI designers, architects, and QA folks. This book was also written for educators who would like to try pair programming with their students. Depending on your role, may we suggest the following process for reading this book:

- Software developers and team leaders/coaches who haven't yet tried pair programming will find Part One very useful. All should read Chapters 1–3 very carefully. If you are trying to convince your manager to transition to pair programming, Chapter 4 will be helpful. If you would like to convince your peers to give pair programming a shot, Chapter 5 is for you. If you are currently being forced into pair programming, Chapter 6 will give you some guidance. Chapter 7 will prepare you for some potential problems you may encounter. Then you can move on to the chapters in Part Two to get into some of the more operational issues you will need to deal with in a transition to pair programming. Chapter 27, "Seven Habits of Effective Pair Programmers," will get you started on the right track. Appendix A, "Pair Programming Tutorial," can be used to help you transition a team or convince a team to take the pair programming plunge.

- Software developers and team leaders/coaches who are currently doing pair programming should start skimming Chapters 1–3. Much of this information will be review for you, but you may pick up some additional insight. Then you can move on to the chapters in Part Two to get into some of the more operational issues. Part Three will be particularly important in guiding you to choosing the best pair for the task at hand. Chapter 27, "Seven Habits of Effective Pair Programmers," will be a good grand finale for you. How many of these habits do you practice? Appendix D provides information about including Test-Driven Development with pair programming.

- QA personnel might be wondering how to handle a development team that has practiced or plans to practice pair programming. Chapters 1–4 will give you a solid understanding of the technique and its benefits. Chapters 10 and 26 also discuss the possibility of pair programming as a substitute to code inspections. Appendix D discusses the composition of pair programming and a testing technique called Test-Driven Development.

- Managers should start by reading Chapters 1–4 and Chapter 7 of Part One. Then, if you are trying to convince a team to try pair programming, Chapter 6 will be helpful. It advises you to run a Pair Programming Tutorial, outlined in Appendix A, with your team. Part Two provides information about operational issues of pair programming, and Chapter 26 provides information on some directions pair programming may lead to.

- Educators should read the first four chapters of Part One to gain a good basic understanding of the technique. Chapters 8, 10, and 11 provide some tactical information about your students. Depending on the skill level and mix of your students, choose some chapters in Part Three. Chapter 26 should appeal to your academic research interests, and Chapter 27 provides good information to share with your students. Appendix C was written with educators in mind and provides some sound tactical advice for using pair programming in the classroom.

Acknowledgments

It seems to me shallow and arrogant for any man in these times to claim he is completely self-made, that he owes all his success to his own unaided efforts. Many hands and hearts and minds generally contribute to anyone's notable achievements.

—Walt Disney

Anyone who knows what a Disney fanatic Bob is will understand how appropriate it is to begin our acknowledgments with a quote from Walt Disney. Undoubtedly, this book would not have been possible without the help of the hands and hearts and minds of many of our friends, family, and respected colleagues.

Laurie: From the bottom of my heart, I thank my family for their unconditional love and support. Thanks to my husband Danny for enduring my complaining ☺, for being my cheerleader, and for watching the kids while I was writing. I could not have done it without you! The absolute and unqualified love of our children, Christopher, Kimberly, and Brian, has always given me great strength. Your smiling eyes help put life back in perspective. I want to thank my parents for their love and support. From childhood, they inspired me always to strive for excellence and gave me a love of learning. I thank God for giving me the ability, confidence, and perseverance to write this book. Last, I want to thank my coauthor and doctoral advisor, Bob Kessler. You have been a wonderful mentor and friend over the last five years. Thanks for writing this book with me and for your tremendous support and encouragement as my advisor.

Laurie would also like to thank her graduate students, Prashant Baheti, Puneet Bheti, Boby George, Anuja Shukla, and Kai Yang, for their research that contributed in a few areas of the book. Thanks to Matt Senter of Senternet IT Consultants (senternet.com) for preparing the second pair programming survey as a class project and experimenting with distributed pair programming. She would also like to thank Hakan Erdogmus for working with her on the thorough economic analysis of Appendix B and to acknowledge her distributed pair programming research partner, Dr. David Stotts at the University of North Carolina, Chapel Hill. Last, she would like to thank Kent Beck, Alistair Cockburn, and Jim Coplien for their support and encouragement in the early days of the pair programming research.

Laurie would also like to mention that the research related to pair programming in the classroom was funded by the National Science Foundation. The NSF has funded research on student pair programming at both North Carolina State University and the University of California, Santa Cruz.

Bob: First of all, I'd like to thank my family. My wife Julie has always supported my professional efforts even though I often stay up too late working. She has juggled her job and the family and has put up with all of the deadlines. Additionally she has always been there to handle the home life when I've been too busy. I also thank our kids, Alex and Chelsea, for helping to enrich and fulfill our lives. I'd like to thank my parents for laying the foundation that has helped me get where I am today. I'd also like to thank Martin Griss for the years of being a great mentor, colleague, and most importantly, a friend. Last, I would be remiss without thanking my coauthor Laurie. It has been a real treat to watch her grow from a brand new graduate student into a highly regarded, professional colleague. It has been a real treat for me to "pair-write" this book with her.

Much of the writing of this book was accomplished while Bob was on sabbatical. Thus, he wants to thank the University of Utah for supporting his sabbatical, plus Hewlett-Packard and Microsoft for providing funding during his sabbatical year.

We would both like to thank our editor, Peter Gordon. We appreciate your unfaltering guidance for making this book as marketable as possible. We'd also like to thank Jacquelyn Doucette, our production editor.

We would also like to thank the many pair programmers who graciously allowed us to reference or quote them in this book: Ken Auer, Fred Brooks, Paul Chisholm, Wayne Conrad, Matthias Felleisen, Dick Gabriel, Bob Hartman, Bil Kleb, Andre McKinlay, Roy Miller, Don Wells, and Bill Wood. In Part Three, we thank all those who contributed the supporting quotes: Kent Beck, Anders Bengtsson, Erik Bennerhult, Jeff Canna, Dave Chaplin, Stu Charlton, Wayne Conrad, Matthew Cooke, Martin Griss, Steve Hayes, Eric Herman, Greg Houston, Ron Jeffries, Todd Jonker, Mike Lance, Jeff Langr, Lee Lichtenwalner, Michael Lindner, Iain Lowe, Tim Mackinnon, Peter Merel, Roy Miller, AK Molteni, Jim Murphy, Vera Peeters, Christian Pekeler, Markus Pfister, Norman Rekitt, Jason Rogers, John Sisk, Stephanie Ward, and Christian Wege.

Last but not, least, we'd like to thank our book reviewers. Thanks for challenging us, correcting us, advising us, complimenting us, and encouraging us: Goerge Burcham, Alistair Cockburn, Steve Hayes, Dave Hendricksen, Ron Jeffries, Tim Mackinnon, Andrew McKinlay, Jim Murphy, Mark Paulk, Leo Scott, Dave Thomas, and Don Wells.

A very special thanks to three reviewers who did incredibly thorough, detailed reading and gave a host of great suggestions: Paul Chisholm, Bil Kleb, and Bill Wood. Last, many thanks to Jim Coplien for kicking our you-know-what. Without your challenges, support, and guidance, this would have been a very different book.

Gaining Understanding

At face value, pair programming is a very simple concept. Two programmers work together at one computer on the same task. Done.

If it was that easy and it worked, that would be all there is to say. There are, however, people and personalities involved. These people and personalities have programmed by themselves for a long time now and need to be convinced that pairing would make things better. Or, they work with peers who think it would be better to work alone. There could be a development team that might consist of heroic "Lone Rangers" who wouldn't get down off their pedestal to share any glory with anyone. There are managers who manage programmers who have always worked alone. Why in the world would he or she want to pair them up, or allow them to pair up if they wanted to? Doubtlessly, a team culture is hard to change.

The purpose of Part One is to help you understand the technique of pair programming from several different perspectives—development, management, QA, and so on. Chapters 1–7 will help you understand the costs, benefits, and complications of transitioning to the technique and help you understand the kinds of things that go on between a pair of programmers who work together.

In the words of Tom DeMarco, "An individual can only succeed to the extent that the whole prospers. And the whole can only prosper to the extent that everyone does well (DeMarco 1995)." The knowledge we share in this section will help you understand how pairing can help your "whole" prosper and to get stated with that culture change.

References

DeMarco, Tom (1995), "The Choir and the Team," *The Dorset House Quarterly*, Nov. 4, 1995, p. 4.

Introduction

Programmers. Professor Matthias Felleisen, formerly at Rice University and now at Northeastern University, has described programmers as, "Lonely macho warriors, battling against a sea of bits and bytes." Programming can be fun—it is creative, complex, and logical. When things go right, we are childishly delighted with what we can create and how we can improve life with our creations. When things go wrong, as they often will, programming can be "bang-your-head-against-the-wall" frustrating. A missing or wrong single character can literally take days to find—we do battle against that sea of bits and bytes. This book is about pair programming, a technique that can radically increase the number of time things go right and decrease the number of times things go wrong. Two programmers, it seems, can more successfully navigate that turbulent sea.

To Pair . . .

Pair programming is a style of programming in which *two* programmers work side by side at one computer, continually collaborating on the same design, algorithm, code, or test. One of the pair, called the *driver*, is typing at the computer or writing down a design. The other partner, called the *navigator,* has many jobs, one of which is to observe the work of the driver, looking for tactical and strategic defects. Tactical defects are syntax errors, typos, calling the wrong method, and so on. Strategic defects occur when the driver is headed down the wrong path—what is implemented just won't accomplish what needs to be accomplished. The navigator is the strategic, long-range thinker. Any of us can be guilty of straying off the path, but a simple, "Can you explain what you're doing?" from the navigator can bring us back to earth. The navigator has a much more objective point of view and can better think strategically about the direction of the work. Another great thing is that the driver and the navigator can brainstorm on-demand at any time. An effective pair programming relationship is very active. The driver and the navigator communicate, if only through guttural utterances (as in, "Huh?"), at least every 45 to 60 seconds. It's also very important to switch roles periodically between the driver and the navigator.

. . . or Not to Pair, This Is the Question

Now that you know about pair programming, you might be wondering why on earth someone would want to pair. We'll be telling you much more about these reasons throughout the book, but now we will give you a preview of the benefits of pair programming that we've seen, experienced, and heard about.

1. **Quality.** Pairs produce code with fewer defects.

2. **Time.** As best we can tell, pairs produce higher-quality code in about half the time as individuals. This shortens your cycle time without impacting your overall budget while giving you superior quality. (We'll examine this benefit in detail in Chapter 4.)

3. **Morale.** Pair programmers are happier programmers. This helps job retention because employees who are having fun are less likely to leave.

4. **Trust and Teamwork.** Pair programmers get to know their teammates much better, which builds trust and improves teamwork.

5. **Knowledge Transfer.** Pair programmers, particularly those who don't pair with the same person all the time, know more about the overall system.

6. **Enhanced learning.** Pairs continoually learn by watching how their partners approach a task, how they use language capabilities, and how they use the development tools.

These benefits apply not only to new code development, but overwhelmingly to code maintenance/enhancement too.

A Fly on the Wall

So, what's it like? To help you envision a development team that practices pair programming, let's be a fly on the wall one morning when a team of developers is getting started. This team practices pair programming and pair rotation (explained in depth in Chapter 9). With pair rotation, the makeup of each pair is very dynamic and depends on the specific tasks that need be done that day (or that week, perhaps). This team begins each day with a short meeting. Everyone stands during these meetings to emphasize just how short the meeting should be. Going around the circle, each person explains what he or she accomplished the day before, if there is anything causing problems, and what needs to be accomplished today. In the XP methodology, these meetings are called "stand-up meetings" (Auer and Miller 2002). In the SCRUM methodology, these are called "SCRUM meetings" (Beedle and Schwaber 2002). These short meetings are excellent for team building and communication as well as to determine who will pair with whom for the day, the morning, or the afternoon.

This following team consists of six developers working on an e-commerce application. As the scene begins, five of them are standing in a circle. Conspicuously, there is a speakerphone on a table near the circle because one team member, Chris, is working from home today. Let's see how it's going as Kimberly, Chris, Brian, Chelsea, Alex, and Julie get started this morning.

Kimberly: Yesterday, Chelsea and I worked on the new account entry form. We finished the form, but now we have some concerns that some of the entries we have on the form might violate our privacy policy.

Julie (*interrupting*): Kimberly, I can work with you this morning to resolve the privacy concerns you have.

Kimberly (*finishing*): That would be awesome, Julie. We could probably finish it up in just a couple of hours this morning. Anyway, Chelsea and I finished the form and the database design to save the data in. Chelsea, maybe this afternoon you and I can make the data-based changes based on the changes that Julie and I come up with this morning.

Chelsea: That's fine. I guess I'll go next then. As Kimberly said, she and I did the new account-entry form and the backend database yesterday. This afternoon, she and I will make the changes to these based on Julie's review of any privacy concerns. That leaves me open to work with someone this morning. I'd like to start working on the JavaScript to verify this form.

Alex: Brian and I just did that for the shopping cart yesterday. I'll be fine helping you with that this morning. Julie, then maybe you can work with me on privacy problems with the shopping cart this afternoon.

Chris (*from the speakerphone*): Sorry, my car didn't start this morning. Good thing I have AAA. The tow truck just picked it up. Anyway, yesterday, I worked with Julie on the privacy policy. You sure know the laws, and you sure know how to protect our customers (and make sure they don't sue our pants off). No offense, Julie, but, geez, everyone in the world's not a lawyer. Real people are supposed to be able to read those policies! So, anyway, Julie and I finished our privacy policy page. Now real people can read it, and the page matches the style of the rest of our site. We sent it off to BBBOnLine for review yesterday afternoon. They should be back to us next Monday. While I'm home, I'd like to work with Brian to overhaul the FAQ page today. Can we work on that in a NetMeeting session, Brian?

Brian: Sure. Like Alex said, he and I worked on form validation for the shopping cart yesterday. Today I guess I'll work with Chris to overhaul the FAQ page. Guess it doesn't live up to your style standards, eh, Chris? (*laughing*)

Chris (*laughing*): No, not quite. Guess we should have paired the first time you developed that!

End of meeting.

Now, the right people are pairing on the right tasks to get the job done, that is, the job of finishing the entire application (not each person's tasks). Everyone disbands to his or her pairing workstations. Brian fires up NetMeeting to work with Chris remotely. (We'll discuss remote pairing further in Chapter 26.) Our fly flies to the top of Alex and Chelsea's monitor. It's a nice large LCD so they can both easily see what's going on. Alex and Chelsea are talking about the form validation for the new account form.

> Chelsea: OK, so we need to validate this form to make sure we send good data onto the database. The first two fields of the form are LastName and FirstName. To be honest, I haven't done this before. I'm thinking that we need to make sure that the user enters letters, not numbers or special characters—no spaces either. Actually, Alex, let's brainstorm a list of all the stupid things that users can do, and then we'll write the functions for each of them.

> Alex: Brian and I did that very same thing yesterday when we did the validation for the shopping cart. Actually, just let me get over to that directory, and I'll find out the name of the file we have all those functions in. Then you can just include that file *(grabs keyboard)*. Here it is. See, we've defined `isWhitespace`, `isDigit`, `isLetter`, `checkString,` and a whole bunch of other functions you'll need for other parts of the form.

> Chelsea *(singing, taking keyboard back)*: Oh, yeah! Oh yeah!

> Chelsea *(typing)*: `<script language="javaScript">`
> `            function validateForm () {`

> Alex: It's probably better if you validate each field separately instead of validating the whole form at one time.

> Chelsea: Well, I thought I could just make one function to validate the whole form, and that function would call a bunch of functions to validate each field. After all, none of the validation takes place until the user hits the "submit" button for the whole form anyway.

> Alex: Yeah, I guess you're right.

> Chelsea *(typing)*: `if (checkStrings(lastName)) then`

> Alex: Actually that function is called `checkString`, not `checkStrings`—there's no s at the end.

> Chelsea: Thanks. Good catch.

Alex and Chelsea's session continues along these lines. There's sharing of whole files (saving hours or days of work), questioning, suggesting, and brainstorming. Without a doubt, by the end of their session, that form will be more correct and more "idiot proof" than if Alex or Chelsea had worked alone. Between the two of them, Alex and Chelsea can think through any mistake that any idiot, er, user could possibly make!

A Pair Programming Timeline

People have advocated and practiced pair programming for decades.

- Fred Brooks, author of *The Mythical Man,* communicated to Laurie in an e-mail, "Fellow graduate student Bill Wright and I first tried pair programming when I was a grad student (1953–56). We produced 1500 lines of defect-free code; it ran correctly first try."

- Dick Gabriel, who conceived of Common Lisp and introduced the concepts of patterns and pattern languages in the software community, reports pair programming in the early 1970s. A historical perspective of his experiences is shared in a sidebar in this chapter.

- In the early 1980s, Larry Constantine, author of more than 150 technical articles and 16 books, reported observing "Dynamic Duos" at Whitesmiths, Ltd., producing code faster and more bug-free than ever before. He commented that the code benefited from the thinking of two bright minds and the steady dialog between two trusted programmers. He concluded that two programmers in tandem was not redundancy, but rather it was a direct route to greater efficiency and better quality (Constantine 1995).

- Based on research finding of the Pasteur project[1] at Bell Labs Research, James Coplien, one of the most influential people in the software patterns movement, published the "Developing in Pairs" Organizational Pattern that same year (1995). Jim identified the forces of this pattern as "People sometimes feel they can solve a problem only if they have help. Some problems are bigger than any one individual." The solution was "Pair compatible designers to work together; together, they can produce more than the sum of the two individually." And the result of applying this pattern is, "A more

---

[1] The Pasteur project extracted empirical structure from over 50 highly effective software development organizations, using data-gathering and analysis techniques similar to those used by sociologists and anthropologists.

effective implementation process. A pair of people is less likely to be blind-sided than an individual developer."

- Author Bob Kessler pair programmed with Martin Griss, coauthor with Ivar Jacobson and Patrick Jonsson of *Software Reuse,* for years before learning there was a name for the technique.

- The largest known group of pair programmers is among an emerging and growing group of programmers that follow the Extreme Programming (XP) methodology developed by Kent Beck (2000), which will be described in Chapter 24. XP has prominently shown us the benefits possible with pair programming.

These reported successes motivated us to research the practice of pair programming. Through extensive groundbreaking study and research (Williams 2000), we've been able to validate statistically the anecdotal claims that pair programming is an affordable means for producing higher quality software. Knowing what we now know about the practice, we can confidently incorporate pair programming into virtually any software development methodology. We've dedicated Part Four to showing you how pair programming fits into two specific development processes and to discussing, in general, the things that need to be considered if you do decide to add it to your process.

Some Words of Caution

We use the word *programming* to include all phases of the development process (design, debugging, testing, and so on), not just coding. So, pair programming would include pair design, pair debugging, pair testing, and so on. In fact, two studies have indicated that pairing is most important for analysis and design (Williams et al. 2000, Allen 2001). We believe people should pair at any time during development, in particular when they are working on something that is complex. The more complex the task, the greater the need for two brains.

One last word of caution before we launch into the book: We really believe that no one should be forced to pair program. We've seen that most people resist transitioning to pair programming—it involves breaking old habits and being more communicative and collaborative than we've been conditioned to be. But among those who try it, almost every single person decides it is better than working alone. We know that there are people out there who would quit their jobs if they were forced to pair. We prefer to think of pair programming as one of those pyramid marketing growth plans . . . let those who are overly enthusiastic pair first. They'll tell their friends how great it is, and their friends will want to try. These friends will tell their friends and . . . you know how it goes.

Ultimately, pair programming is not for all. Solo programmers can always contribute to our teams.

References

Allen, Adrian. "An Investigation into Potential Reasons Why Pair Programming is Not Widely Adopted by Programmers as a Standard Development Practice When Developing Software," Technical Report, University of Cape Town, October 2001.

Auer, K. and Miller, R. (2002). *Extreme Programming Applied: Playing to Win*, Addison-Wesley.

Beck, K. (2000). *Extreme Programming Explained: Embrace Change*, Addison-Wesley.

Beedle, M. and Schwaber, K. (2001). *Agile Software Development with SCRUM*, Prentice Hall.

Brooks, F. P. (1995). *The Mythical Man Month: Anniversary Edition*, Addison-Wesley.

Constantine, L. L. (1995). *Constantine on Peopleware*, Yourdon Press.

Coplien, J. O. (1995). "A Development Process Generative Pattern Language," in *Pattern Languages of Program Design*, James O. Coplien and Douglas C. Schmidt, eds., Addison-Wesley, 183–237.

Williams, L. A. (2000). "The Collaborative Software Process," Ph.D. dissertation, University of Utah.

Williams, L., Kessler, R., Cunningham, W., and Jeffries, R. (2000). "Strengthening the Case for Pair-Programming." *IEEE Software*, July/August 2000, 19–25.

A Personal Historical Account of Pair Programming
by Dick Gabriel

Pair programming was a common practice at the M.I.T. Artificial Intelligence Laboratory when I was there in 1972–73. Later, when I was at the University of Illinois and at Stanford University, I would pair program with Jonl White while trying to adapt the M.I.T. Lisp system, MacLisp, to the operating systems I was using at those schools. Jonl would visit, or I would go back to Cambridge, and we'd sit next to each other in front of his or my terminal. The driver would be whichever one of us was more familiar with the code being worked on. Remember: We were adding to and altering an existing large system.

In 1984 I started Lucid, and we began planning how to do an implementation of Common Lisp in nine months. We hired Martin Brooks as a consultant to help define the process. Each of the fifteen developers took responsibility for a number of modules, which were large pieces of functionality that could be worked on separately; for example, I took the memory management module. Other modules included the compiler, the interpreter, mapping functions, arrays, a debugger, and so on. The modules were not necessarily disjointed because of the nature of the planned implementation. Each module was also assigned a buddy who worked very closely with the module owner. The arc of development for each module was the same: first, a design plan in writing, then implementation and test plans in writing, then coding both the module and the tests, and finally integration. Integrations took place frequently—sometimes one or more times a day—once we got going.

The module owner and buddy wrote the plans together, although the owner did most of the writing. The entire development group reviewed and approved each plan before implementation started. The coding was sometimes done entirely in pairs, but usually there would be stretches as long as a day or two at a time when the owner would type in code alone. However, at most the buddy reviewed each line of code within a day of its creation. Small review boards drawn from the development group reviewed each implementation line-by-line before integration.

The entire development group met frequently as well to report general progress. Usually there was an informal all-hands meeting every day, usually over lunch, with a formal meeting every week.

The buddy system worked very much as pair programming does today; the main exception was that the buddy would not always be sitting next to the module owner, although I can't recall a day when a module owner and a buddy didn't work together. Each buddy was also a module owner, sometimes the owner of several modules, and he or she would have other buddies to work with. This process can be viewed as an exercise in scaling classical pair programming to a large project.

The reasons we used the buddy system included the usual ones stated for pair programming, but they also included the need for each module to have a second person who could step in if the module owner became incapacitated— we literally feared the hit-by-a-truck scenario. Further, we needed to do a commercial delivery of a half-million line system with strict quality requirements in nine months—hence the need for developing tests alongwith the module code. On the other hand, each of the fifteen developers had already written parts or all of a Lisp system several times in his or her career.

I've also written several technical papers using pair writing. It's exactly like programming, but the pair is writing text. "The Evolution of Lisp" by Guy L. Steele, Jr. and myself in *History of Programming Languages II,* edited by Thomas J. Bergin and Richard G. Gibson, was written this way.

The Seven Myths of Pair Programming

Often people who have not tried pair programming are hesitant to start or to encourage others to start. Resistance to transitioning to pair programming comes from both the top down (from management) and from the bottom up (from engineers). It's hard to foster support for a new practice with resistance coming from both sides! Often, though, the resistance comes from misconceptions from those who have never tried it, based on reasonable and rational, but incorrect, assumptions.

In this chapter, we will go through these common misconceptions that we've heard about concerning pair programming. We'll also dig deeper into most of these myths in coming chapters.

Myth 1: It will double the workload with two doing the work one can do.

Managers say, "Pair programming increases the cost of development. We can't afford that!"

Software engineers say, "When I signed up to do my tasks, I didn't leave extra time for helping other people do their work."

We became interested in pair programming after hearing Extreme Programmers' wonderful stories of success with the technique. Prior to the publication of *Extreme Programming Explained* (Beck 2000), XP's first book, Ward Cunningham's *Portland Pattern Repository* was the prime communication vehicle for the definition of the XP methodology. On Ward's Wiki we read, "Get two people programming in pairs, and they'll work more than twice as fast as one could have" (Wiki 1999, contributed by Paul Chisholm). We also read, "One of the rules of the Chrysler Comprehensive Compensation team is that all production code be written with a partner. As a testimonial, in the last six months before launching, the only code that caused problems was code written solo" (Wiki 1999, contributed by Kent Beck). Could that be true? If it is true, then the concerns of the manager and the software engineers mentioned earlier disappear. In addition to being academics, we both have been heavily involved in commercial software development, and so we could sympathize with the concerns. We were intrigued; we wanted to know if it was really true.

To validate the anecdotal claims we were hearing, we ran a formal experiment with 41 students writing four programs over a 16-week semester at the University of Utah. When these solo and pair programmers "competed" head-to-head, the pair programmers finished in about half the time as solo programmers, and there were fewer defects.

For many, this myth alone is a stopper. If this is the case with you, we encourage you to flip to Chapter 4 for a full discussion on the economics of pair programming.

Myth 2: I'll never get to work alone. I couldn't stand that!

Extreme Programmers (XPers) believe in pair programming so much that any production code done alone needs to be redone with a partner. Many practicing pair programmers take a more moderate approach to pair programming. We ran a survey that was advertised on pair programming and XP mailing lists. We also sent personal invitations to participate to every pair programmer we could think of. Only 22 percent of those who took the survey said they spent 75 percent or more of their day pair programming. A full 30 percent said they spend less than half their day pair programming. Pair programmers generally do work alone for a certain period each day. These survey results are consistent with developers in general. In *Peopleware* (DeMarco and Lister 1987), it was reported that software developers generally spend 30 percent of their time working alone, 50 percent of their time working with one other person, and 20 percent of their time working with two or more people. So, historically, developers have collaborated, and pair programming puts some structure around this collaboration.

Pair programming is very intense—too intense for many to do all day every day—and there are schedule constraints to deal with—flex hours, sick partners, meetings, and so on. The advice we give is this: If you don't want to work together at all times, work together on the most complex tasks. Have designated "pair programming hours" in the morning and/or afternoon. At that time, everyone pairs, and no one interrupts. During other hours, work on less complex tasks, go to meetings, and return all the phone calls and e-mails you've been avoiding.

Besides that, you might actually find that you can stand to work with someone else often. In "The Danger of Coding Alone" in *Extreme Programming Applied* (Auer and Miller 2002), Ken Auer describes when he lost quite a few minutes because he deleted what he believed was "superfluous" code while his partner stepped away. (Fortunately there was a test case that revealed the problem.) Actually many pair programmers do report that they really do feel somewhat uncomfortable working alone once they are conditioned to working with a partner. However, situations like a sick, busy, or vacationing teammate will make solo programming necessary. We've done it before; we can do it again.

Myth 3: It will work well *only* with the right partner.

Actually, what we have found is that it will work well with most (admittedly, not all) partners. There seems to be one kind of person that everyone has trouble working with—somone with excess ego and/or a "my way or the highway" attitude. Other than that, people are able to work with almost anyone. One exception might be pairing an expert with a novice. The expert needs to be willing to take on the mentor role—for the good of the long term team performance—knowing that his or her own productivity will be impacted. If an expert does not have these nurturing instincts, it is best not to pair him or her with a novice, as we'll discuss in Chapter 14.

We'll be explaining more about pair rotation in Chapter 9. For now, we'll say that with pair rotation, people pair with different people all the time. Of those we surveyed, 83 percent said they rotate their pairs. We've heard of groups that practice pair rotation with their pairs sticking together for as short as a few hours to as long as a few weeks. However, you don't have to imagine spending the rest of the project shoulder-to-shoulder with one individual. In most cases, people who spend lots of time together (even married couples) can get on each other's nerves. It really helps to know that if you can just make it until (specify day/time), you won't have to work with that person again for awhile.

Myth 4: Pair programming is good for training. But, once you know what you're doing, it is a waste of time.

There is certainly benefit to the apprentice relationship that can take place between a new person and an experienced person. However, pair programming is mutually beneficial to experienced programmers too. Part Three of this book explains the benefits and shortcomings of twelve different kinds of pairs and the contexts in which each kind of pair works best.

Here's a preview of two of the twelve kinds of pairs we discuss in Part Three:

- If you pair two experts when you've got a really complex problem to solve, they will do the best job imaginable. Because each is probably an expert in a slightly or very different area, the synergy of their expertise will bring results.

- If you pair any two experienced programmers, they will fill in many of each other's knowledge gaps. Between the two of them, they can piece together the solution to almost any problem, including problems they would have struggled with alone. This is also a great knowledge management strategy—an excellent way to pass tacit knowledge around a team. Turn to Chapter 9 if you're particularly interested in pair programming and knowledge management.

Myth 5: I'll never get credit for doing anything. I'll have to share all the recognition with my partner.

Recognition gets a bit more complicated when pair programming and pair rotation enter the picture. No longer can you say, "Didn't Kimberly do an excellent job on the storage manager?" Kimberly had help!

We'll approach this myth from two angles. First, things work best if each task has an owner. For example, let's say that Kimberly owns the storage manager and Christopher owns the heap. The owner "recruits" a partner to work with on various parts of the task. It works best if the partner has some related knowledge he or she can bring to the task. For example, when Kimberly is doing the part of the storage manager that interacts with the heap, it would be great if Christopher would work with her. He brings related knowledge to the table and leaves with knowledge about the storage manager. Ultimately, Kimberly can still feel great about her storage manger—partly because she recruited the right teammate to pair with her on the right task (a skill in itself).

But with pairing, much of our time is now spent on tasks we don't own. How can we feel good about that? How can Christopher get satisfaction from helping Kimberly with her storage manager? First, we need to transition to getting more satisfaction from our team succeeding. As with any team, including any sports team, individual success means nothing without team success. We need to realize that we are personally gaining from understanding the overall system much better, which helps us do our own tasks better too.

Having said all this, we recommend that some form of peer evaluation scheme be developed. Peer evaluation can provide valuable feedback to the manager on how helpful the engineers are as partners so the manager has a better idea of whom to reward. Periodically engineers should write a short statement about those team members they have paired with and how effectively they feel the pairing has gone. This will be discussed further in Chapter 10.

Myth 6: The navigator finds only syntax mistakes. How boring is that! Compilers can do that better than humans can anyway.

True, a major benefit of pair programming is the continual code review; the navigator can find syntax mistakes as they are created (although we strongly encourage you to give drivers more than a handful of nanoseconds to fix their own syntax mistakes). However, the job of the navigator is much more important and exciting than this. The navigator is holding the roadmap and is guiding the driver to the desired destination. Sometimes drivers can get so caught up with staying between the lines on a winding road (especially on a snowy night), they forget where they are headed. The navigator can't go to sleep, or the driver might end up lost or worse—he might arrive safely at the wrong destination.

Effective pairing relationships involve two very alert participants. They brainstorm and discuss approaches continuously, and, sometimes they find syntax mistakes in the process.

Myth 7: The only time I ever get any real work done is when I'm alone. Now, I'll never get anything done! Pair programming would drive me crazy.

In *Peopleware*, DeMarco and Lister (1987) describe mental flow:

> Flow is a condition of deep, nearly meditative involvement. In this state, there is a gentle sense of euphoria, and one is largely unaware of the passage of time. . . . There is no consciousness of effort; the work just seems to, well, flow. . . . Not all work roles require that you attain a state of flow in order to be productive, but for anyone involved in engineering, design, development, writing, or similar tasks, flow is a must. These are high-momentum tasks. It's only when you're in a flow that work goes well.

DeMarco and Lister then explain that it takes at least 15 minutes of concentration to slowly "descend" to flow. They say, however, that you can be knocked out of flow by any interruption, such as a phone call or that ever-present e-mail ding. Every time you are interrupted, it takes another 15 minutes to get back into flow.

People who have never pair programmed worry that they will never reach this euphoric flow state when working with another who, for example, just won't stop talking and whose job it is, in fact, to talk. However, many of those who have tried pair programming have experienced the "two heads are better than one" version of mental flow. The two operate as one intelligent organism and share an enhanced, joint flow. Together they explore more possibilities and revel in their joint successes. They know from minute to minute that they are achieving more together than they ever could alone, and this knowledge drives them deeper and deeper into flow. Pairs can also prevent each other from flowing down the wrong river by productively producing the wrong thing or low-quality code.

When pairs work together, they do a much better job at deferring interruptions. They forward their phone to voicemail, they turn off their e-mail notification, and they don't take "surf the Web" breaks. When other people walk by and see them working, they often choose not to interrupt. Actually pairs also report that if they are jointly in the flow state and one of the pair is interrupted, the interrupted partner can quickly rejoin the flow of the partner who continued—without DeMarco and Lister's 15-minute "descent" time. At the end of a session, they return to the real world and handle all the voice-mails, e-mail, and so on.

The opposite of mental flow is mental block (or distraction). Pair programming reduces this obstruction either because the pairs keep each other on track (and are not distracted) or because one of the pair is able to break through the mental block. Often, either one of the pair can at least start any task, no matter how impossible it seems initially.

As we'll discuss in Chapter 4, almost all (well over 90 percent of those surveyed) say that they enjoy programming more and feel more confident in their work when they pair program.

References

Auer, K. and Miller, R. (2002). *Extreme Programming Applied: Playing to Win*, Addison-Wesley.

Beck, K. (2000). *Extreme Programming Explained: Embrace Change*, Addison-Wesley.

DeMarco, T. and Lister, T. (1987). *Peopleware*, Dorset House Publishers.

Kelley, R. E. (1985). *The Gold Collar Worker: Harnessing the Brain Power of the New Workforce*, Addison-Wesley.

Wiki. (1999). "Pair Programming," Portland Pattern Repository, http://c2.com/cgi/wiki?PairProgramming.

The Seven Synergistic Behaviors of Pair Programming

Two software engineers sit down at one computer and work on one task. They finish essentially twice as fast as if either one of them had done the task alone. And, they have higher quality work! How can this be? Is this some kind of voodoo magic? Are we exploiting some aspects of human nature?

Pairing actually does make us work differently. Observing effective pairs, we've identified seven synergistic behaviors. These behaviors tend to happen "naturally" with pairs, as opposed to the habits of effective pair programmers in Chapter 27, which can take practice and concerted effort. Working together synergistically, we get our jobs done faster and better with these behaviors and without us feeling uptight about it. The more of these behaviors a pair allows to emerge, the more effective the pair will be.

In fact, we could add an eighth behavior, *pair fun*. In our recent Web survey, we asked, "What have you found beneficial about pair programming?" The single most common response was, "It's a lot more fun!"

Behavior 1: Pair Pressure

Pair programmers put a positive form of pressure on each other. This pair pressure causes us to react in several ways.

Programmers admit to working harder and smarter on programs because they do not want to let their partner down.

We'll illustrate this phenomenon by comparing two scenarios.

Scenario One: Last night, for example, North Carolina State played the University of North Carolina in a basketball game. Your neighbor, who has center-court tickets only ten rows from the floor, took you to the game. In overtime, North Carolina State (your team, and the underdog) comes out on top; it was a nail biter! There's one small problem, though: after a couple of victory beverages, you don't get home until well after midnight, and you have to get up at the crack of dawn to take your son to swim practice before school. You get to work and chat at the coffee machine a bit too long (razzing your UNC colleagues about the game, of course). When you finally make it to your desk, lack of sleep sets in. After several minutes of staring blankly at your screen, you decide to find out if it's going to rain on Saturday, you just have to send e-mails to all the rest of the UNC fans you know. You hit "send" on that one final note and then stare at the screen for a few more minutes. Just as you're starting up Visual Age, the phone rings. Happy Day! It's your college buddy, Danny, calling to plan your houseboat vacation on Lake Powell in southern Utah.

Scenario Two: Last night, your best friend just announced he got engaged. He's the first one "to go." You know your girlfriend will start looking at you funny now, but for tonight . . . parrrrrty!

This morning you perform complex analysis on your alarm clock to figure out just how many times you could hit the snooze alarm and still get to work on time. You slowly walk from the parking lot to the building. As you walk down the hallway toward your cube, you see Chris walking toward you for your 8:30 pairing session. (He never stops smiling, does he?) The two of you are scheduled to finish the print spooler before noon. As you unlock your desk, he's starting up the computer. You strategically position your Big Slurpee of Mountain Dew and sit down next to Chris. Let the day begin!

When you're working alone, you can (intentionally or unintentionally) hide in your cube and waste time on mindless tasks. Simply the presence of another can draw us out of our tired, disgruntled mood and cause us to get to work. As we'll discuss in the next chapter, Laurie has compared the results of her students who pair program and those who do not. Students who pair perform much more consistently (and better) than those who don't. We just don't want to let the person next to us down, or we're embarrassed to disappoint him or her or look like a slacker.

When programmers meet with their partner, they both work very intensively because they are highly motivated to complete the task at hand during the session.

"Two people working together in a pair treat their shared time as more valuable. They tend to cut phone calls short; they don't check e-mail messages or favorite Web pages; they don't waste each other's time" (Wiki 1999, contributed by Paul Chisholm).

When we work alone, we can meander through the day. We can get ourselves into that mental state we call flow when we want; We can surf the Web when we want; We go to meetings and to lunch when we want.

Things are different when we pair. When we pair, we need to coordinate schedules. (This is something that some people don't like about pair programming.) Your partner, Alex, needs to drop his kids off at school before coming in. You prefer to get in early so you can get to the gym in the afternoon before the mad rush. That leaves 9–3 as the only possible pairing hours, but, then there's lunch and a meeting or two. So, that leaves only 9–11 and 1–3. That leaves only four hours, and you need to have the socket code done by the end of the day. During these precious four hours, you're motivated to work intensively to get to the goal line by the end of the day. You know that Alex needs to pair with Chelsea tomorrow, and you won't have his expertise anymore.

Parkinson's Law (Parkinson 1958) helps to explain this phenomenon. This law states, "Work expands to fill the time available." If you have four hours together to finish that socket code today, you'll get it done. When you work alone, you generally don't put such explicit, externally visible deadlines on yourself. If you could finish before lunch but don't have your afternoon planned out, your task might expand to take the whole day. Pairing continually provides explicit deadlines that motivate us to finish the task and not let it fill any "extra" time.

In *Peopleware* (DeMarco and Lister 1987), the authors enumerate the "Environmental Factor" or E-Factor as:

$$\text{E-Factor} = \frac{\text{Uninterrupted Hours}}{\text{Body-Present Hours}}$$

The higher the E-Factor, the more productive programmers are. We work very intently because we value our time with our partner. We purposely won't answer our phone or e-mails. Others see us already working with someone else, and they leave us alone. The net effect is that we have bigger blocks of uninterrupted time, which is good for our mental state and our progress. It also reduces task switching, which for some people generates a huge overhead.

Are pairs the only ones that can turn off interruptions? Of course not! Many time management strategies, including that found in the *Gold Collar Worker* (Kelley 1985), will advise turning off the phone and ignoring the inbox to focus on the task at hand. It has been demonstrated (DeMarco and Lister 1987) that programmers who have the ability to silence their phone and divert their calls and have fewer interruptions can be far more productive (as much as eleven times faster). It's just that with a partner depending on us, we're less likely to "cheat."

> **With any software development process there is a constant struggle to get the software engineers to follow the prescribed process. A benefit of pair pressure is improved adherence to procedures and standards.**

Due to human nature, pairs put a positive form of pressure on each other to follow the prescribed process. Agile processes (Cockburn 2002) can have practices that are quite "lightweight" and minimal in order to maximize a team's ability to be responsive. If these minimal processes are ignored, things could fall apart. Together, pairs more consistently adhere to prescribed practices and, therefore, produce with higher quality results (after all, the creators of the process include all the practices for a reason). Each partner expects the other to follow the prescribed development practices and acts as a conscience to the other. "With your partner watching, though, chances are that even if you feel like blowing off one of these practices, your partner won't . . . the chances of ignoring your commitment to the rest of the team is much smaller in pairs then it is when you work alone" (Beck 2000).

Behavior 2: Pair Negotiation

Anyone who has closely observed the practices of cognition is struck by the fact that the "mind" rarely works alone. The intelligences revealed through these practices are distributed—across minds, persons, and the symbolic and physical environment. . . . Knowledge is commonly socially constructed, through collaborative efforts toward shared objectives or by dialogues and challenges brought about by differences in persons' perspectives. (Salomon 1993)

The second of the pair programming behaviors we discuss is pair negotiation. We use the term *pair negotiation* to describe how two pair programmers arrive at the best solution together. Pair negotiation is grounded in an area of psychology called *distributed cognition*. Specifically, Flor and Hutchins (1991) studied the exchanges of two programmers working together on a software maintenance task. They correlated specific verbal and nonverbal behaviors of the two with known distributed cognition theories. When pairing is working at its best,

- Each brings to the pair partnership his or her own set of skills, abilities, and outlook.

- Both share the same goal for completing the task.

- They jointly approach a problem, each with a suggested alternative for attacking it.

- They must "negotiate" how to approach the problem jointly. In this negotiation, they evaluate more alternatives than either one would have considered alone; a person working alone tends to pursue his or her first approach.

- Together, the pair efficiently determines which is the best plan of attack, considering and including suggestions from both partners.

- They "high five" each other for being so smart and kicking butt on the task. (We must admit we found nothing in the distributed cognition literature about this last step, but we know it to be true.)

Some people are concerned that the negotiation might lead to "worst of both worlds" compromises in implementation. Two studies investigate whether group decision making is superior to the decisions of the more knowledgeable member. Michaelsen et al. (1989) studied 222 teams involved in 25 organizational behavior courses. First, each completed each test individually; then the teams completed the test collaboratively. All 222 groups outperformed their average member, and 215 groups outperformed their best member. As a follow-up study, Watson et al. (1991), determined that the longer a group works together, the better their decision-making effectiveness.

Finally, decision issues fall on a continuum from purely judgmental (no correct answers exist) to purely intellective (those that have a demonstrably correct answer). Software correctness decisions are almost always intellective. Groups will generally form a consensus on judgmental decisions and will generally produce the correct answer to an intellective issue if any member of the group proposes it (Hungerford and Hevner 1997). Therefore the synergistic effects arising from programming in pairs are partly due to one of the pair proposing the "correct answer" during the work time; this answer might not have been identified if one worked alone.

Related to pair negotiation, collaborative teams consistently report that together they can evolve solutions to unruly or seemingly impossible problems. *Pair brainstorming* is the effect of having two people working to resolve a problem together. They share their knowledge and energy, chipping steadily away at the problem, evolving a solution to the problem. An effective brainstorming technique (Morgan 1993) is to encourage people to build upon the ideas of others. A subtle difference though, is that the driver might actually be working out a design or implementing part of the problem, realizing that he or she may ultimately come to a dead end in the problem resolution. The navigator, while watching the driver's partial design or implementation, begins thinking about the next step. When the driver hits the dead end, the navigator is often prepared to take over and lead the way. Often, the cycle continues until the problem is resolved.

Behavior 3: Pair Courage

Having a partner is a tremendous courage builder. You can say to each other, "Does this look right to you?" "Do you think this part needs to be refactored?" Getting affirmation from our partner gives us the confidence to do things we might be afraid to do alone or simply might avoid and never do. As teachers, we witness this every day. If you give students a problem, ask them to solve it during class, and ask them for the answer, you'll be guaranteed to get a room full of blank stares with the same two or three hands raised. Most people will avoid sharing their answer because they don't want to look stupid if they are wrong. If you tell the students to work out the problem with their neighbor and then ask for input, nearly every pair will willingly share their answer.

When we work with someone else, we can piece together enough knowledge to feel confident in what we're doing. And, if it looks right to me and it looks right to you—guess what—it's probably right! Strength in numbers!

Pairing also gives us courage to admit when we don't know something. Developers by themselves tend to be embarrassed when they don't know something and will try to muddle through on their own rather than ask for help from their peers. A study done at the University of Cape Town revealed that 42 percent of developers are inclined to work on problems alone rather than ask for help. Interestingly enough, the more experience a developer has, the more likely he or she is to ask for help; novices are less likely to ask for help (Allen 2001). When two people don't know something, there is a joint realization that it is time to seek help from their peers who may have experience in the problem area.

Behavior 4: Pair Reviews

Inspections were introduced more than 20 years ago as a cost-effective means of detecting and removing defects from software. Results from empirical studies (Fagan 1976) consistently profess the effectiveness of reviews. However, most programmers do not find inspections enjoyable or satisfying. As a result, inspections are often not done if not mandated, and many inspections are held with unprepared inspectors. For example, an informal USENET survey conducted at the University of Hawaii found that 80 percent of 90 respondents practiced inspection irregularly or not at all (Johnson 1998).

The theory on why inspections are effective is based on the prominent knowledge that the earlier a defect is found in a product, the cheaper it is to fix the defect. With pair programming, this problem identification occurs on a minute-by-minute basis. "The human eye has an almost infinite capacity for not seeing what it does not want to see. . . . Programmers, if left to their own devices, will ignore the most glaring errors in their output—errors that anyone else can see in an instant" (Weinberg 1998). With pair programming, "four eyeballs are better than two," and a momentous number of defects are prevented, removed right from the start. These continual reviews outperform traditional, formal reviews in their defect-removal speed. Additionally, they eliminate the programmer's distaste for reviews since the reviews are implicit in what is typically an enjoyable pair-programming session.

Behavior 5: Pair Debugging

Every person has experienced problems that can be resolved simply through the act of explaining them to another.

> . . . [An] effective technique is to explain your code to someone else. This will often cause you to explain the bug to yourself. Sometimes it takes no more than a few sentences, followed by an embarassed, "Never mind; I see what's wrong. Sorry to bother you." This works remarkably well; you can even use nonprogrammers as listeners. One university computer center kept a teddy bear near the help desk. Students with mysterious bugs were required to explain them to the teddy bear before they could speak to a human counselor (Kernighan and Pike 1999).

Others have cited the need just to have a cardboard cutout of their favorite guru (Wiki 2001) or a rubber duck (Hunt and Thomas 2000). When they have a problem, they must explain the problem to the cardboard cutout or rubber duck, often finding the flaw in their logic.

Doubtless, it is better to have an animate person to debug with than a teddy bear, rubber duck, or cardboard guru. A person will ask questions and will likely cause you to do the explaining often. The questions and answer can lead to great revelations. Don Wells shares an experience.

> She was working on code I had never seen before on a system I had never seen before. She told me she had a dilemma and wanted to pair program to debug it. She had been working on it for a long time, and it had spoiled her demonstration that morning. She needed to fix the obvious flaw and release the code. I was a bit concerned that I didn't know anything but proceeded, assuming I would be her teddy bear. She explained the problem completely to me; no solution presented itself. So I began asking questions and formulating scenarios with her. We checked each out in turn, and in a few minutes we solved the problem and fixed the code. Let some teddy bear try that.

Behavior 6: Pair Learning

Knowledge is constantly being passed between partners, from tool usage tips to programming language rules to design and programming idioms. The partners take turns being the teacher and the student. Even unspoken skills and habits cross partners (Cockburn and Williams 2001).

Lave and Wenger (1991) have studied various types of apprenticeship. They stress the importance of an apprentice to participate actively, to have legitimate work to do, and to work on the periphery, steadily moving toward some higher rank. The novice's work is initially simple and noncritical. Later work is more critical. Lave and Wenger stress the importance of the apprentice working within a "line of sight" of the expert. The beginner explicitly acquires skills from hearing and/or seeing the expert. To further this, Alistair Cockburn, whose work includes examining practices and patterns that tend to lead toward project success or failure, created the "Expert-in-Earshot" project management pattern. Experts are put in the same workspace as novices so that the novices can learn by watching and listening while the expert does his or her usual work (Cockburn and Williams 2001). In these contexts, pair programming is a much improved apprenticeship situation than a more traditional situation whereby a novice sits in his or her own workspace, working on simple code, while the expert creates complex code elsewhere.

The continuous reviews of collaborative programming create a unique educational capability because the pairs are endlessly learning from each other. "The process of analyzing and critiquing software artifacts produced by others is a potent method for learning about languages, application domains, and so forth" (Johnson 1998). The learning that transcends these continual reviews prevents future defects from occurring—and defect prevention is more efficient than any form of defect removal. The continual reviews of collaborative programming, in which both partners ceaselessly work to identify and resolve problems, affords both optimum defect-removal efficiency and the development of defect-prevention skills.

We'll talk more about pairs swapping with other pairs in Chapter 9, but for now we'll say that when pairs move around and everyone gets to work with everyone else, even more learning occurs, and it occurs at a higher pace. Kent Beck (2000) describes this: "When an important new bit of information is learned by someone on the team, it is like putting a drop of dye in the water.

Because of the pairs switching around all the time, the information rapidly diffuses throughout the team just as the dye spreads throughout the pool. Unlike the dye, however, the information becomes richer and more intense as it spreads and is enriched by the experience and insight of everyone on the team."

If you are interested in the pair learning that can take place among students learning a programming language, read Appendix C.

Behavior 7: Pair Trust

Pairs must also trust each other. Those who program in pairs are developing for the good of the company, not just for themselves. Pairing allows them to open up to other people's knowledge and experience and to see that the end result is far better than anything they could have developed on their own. This in turn allows them to present their best ideas in a more open environment. If the makeup of the pairs is dynamic, developers get to know and trust all (or many) on their team. The trust that develops throughout the team is highly beneficial for the team itself.

These seven behaviors synergistically work together, allowing 2 > 1 + 1. The results of the two together are greater than the results of each individually. And, as we said, the overwhelming sentiment is that it's a lot more fun!

References

Allen, A. (2001). "An Investigation into Potential Reasons Why Pair Programming Is Not Widely Adopted by Programmers as a Standard Development Practice When Developing Software," Technical Report, University of Cape Town, October 2001.

Beck, K. (2000). *Extreme Programming Explained: Embrace Change*, Addison-Wesley.

Cockburn, A. and Williams, L. (2001). "The Costs and Benefits of Pair Programming," in *Extreme Programming Examined,* G. Succi and M. Marches, eds., Addison-Wesley.

DeMarco, T. and Lister, T. (1987). *Peopleware*, Dorset House Publishers.

Fagan, M. E. (1976). "Advances in Software Inspections to Reduce Errors in Program Development." *IBM Systems Journal*, 15: 182–211.

Flor, N. V. and Hutchins, E. L. (1991). "Analyzing Distributed Cognition in Software Teams: A Case Study of Team Programming During Perfective Software Maintenance," *Empirical Studies of Programmers: Fourth Workshop*, 36–63.

Hungerford, B. C. and Hevner, A. R. (1997). "Team Synergy in Software Inspections: A Group Behavior Analysis," Americas Conference on Information Systems.

Hunt, A. and Thomas, D. (2000). *The Pragmatic Programmer: From Journeymen to Master*, Addison-Wesley.

Johnson, P. M. (1998). "Reengineering Inspection: The Future of Formal Technical Review." *Communications of the ACM*, 49–52.

Kernighan, B. W. and Pike, R. (1999). *The Practice of Programming*, Addison-Wesley.

Lave, J. and Wenger, E. (1991). *Situated Learning: Legitimate Peripheral Participation*, Cambridge University Press.

Michaelsen, L., Watson, W., et al. (1989). "Realistic Test of Individual versus Group Decision Making," *Journal of Applied Psychology* 74(5): 834–839.

Morgan, M. (1993). *Creative Workforce Innovation*, Business and Professional Publishing.

Parkinson, C. N. (1958). *Parkinson's Law: The Pursuit of Progress*, The Heretical Press.

Salomon, G. (1993). *Distributed Cognitions: Psychological and Educational Considerations*, Cambridge University Press.

Watson, W., Michaelsen, L., et al. (1991). "Member Competence, Group Interaction, and Group Decision Making: A Longitudinal Study," *Journal of Applied Psychology* 76(6): 803–809.

Weinberg, G. M. (1998). *The Psychology of Computer Programming, Silver Anniversary Edition*, Dorset House Publishing.

Wiki. (1999). "Pair Programming." Portland Pattern Repository, http://c2.com/cgi/wiki?PairProgramming.

Wiki. (2001). "Cardboard Programmer." Portland Pattern Repository, http://c2.com/cgi/wiki?CardboardProgrammer.

Overcoming Management Resistance to Pair Programming

Software development managers often have the knee-jerk reaction "Why in the world would I pay two programmers to do something that one programmer could do?" This is not a surprising reaction.

In this chapter, we're talking to two distinct audiences. First, we're talking to programmers who would really like to get their team into pair programming. We'll give you some "ammunition" as you appeal to your manager's motivations. Second, we're talking to the managers who are trying to decide whether to give it a go. We aim to give you some data that you can use in making that decision.

There are also two levels of pair programming: One is a very casual, noninvasive use of the practice. You and your peer work together a lot, and you both manage to get your job done. You seek out someone to work with you when you have something difficult to do. You offer to help your peers when they have a tough time. We're not going to address this casual use of pair programming in this chapter.

Rather, we're addressing the prevalent use of pair programming throughout a team, where pairing is an integral part of the team dynamics and the team development practices—the kind of use that a manager would generally be aware of. Hopefully, the manager strives to have an "I don't care how you do it, just do it" attitude. But, we know that at the end of the day each manager has a set of objectives that needs to be met so the manager can be relatively assured of being able to feed his or her family. Managers need to know that pairing will help them achieve their objectives.

You might be concerned that no matter what we say, it will double the amount of time you spend on a task, and you can't afford that risk. To you, our recommendation is to have a very small, minimal-risk pilot. Laurie was working with a development team at IBM. She had already told them much of what is included in this chapter. Then she had a meeting with the manager and six of the employees in the department who were interested in trying pair programming. When it really came down to getting started, all were nervous. She encouraged them to pick only two from among them to pair program for only one week. They would treat this as a pilot and see how it went.

This was a minimal-risk pilot that couldn't set a schedule too far back, one person-week at most. By the second day of the pilot, they e-mailed, "It's incredible how much we're teaching each other about our areas of the project." At the end of the week, they had completed a task they estimated at 90 hours in only 60 hours, so they did it in less, not more, time by pairing. This module went on to test with only two reported test defects—one of them occurred during the 10 hours that one of the pair worked alone. One of the programmers commented on the defects, "They could have been caught by [partner] and me during our initial design, code, and debugging, but they weren't because of our inexperience with the function we were providing. They could have been caught by the formal code review we had and fixed before testing found them, but they weren't. No one at the code review asked questions about the areas of the code where the defects occurred."

Pilot experiences like these can give a team more confidence in trying pair programming on a larger scale.

Motivations

When she worked at IBM, Laurie used to teach a class called "Increasing Human Effectiveness." (The Edge Learning Institute developed the course.) Throughout the course, we learned that whenever you set a goal, you should also write down "What's In It For Me" (WIIFM). The only way you'll change your behavior to reach your goal is if there's something in it for you, something you personally gain by changing the behavior. So we consider the goals of you and/or your manager to appeal to the WIIFM thoughts. What are those goals?

1. I want to complete my projects on time with high-quality code.

2. I want to reduce my risk of losing a key person.

3. I want my employees to be happy.

4. I want to reduce the amount of time it takes to train a new person.

5. I want my teams to work well together and to communicate more effectively and efficiently with each other.

Throughout the rest of the chapter, we'll explain our findings in each of these areas. Some of our results are quantitative and some are qualitative.

Goal: I want to complete my projects on time with high-quality code.

WIIFM: My bosses are happier because our business objectives are met or exceeded and because we have improved customer satisfaction.

We need to build the case that the use of pair programming can help managers complete their projects on time and with high quality, a case that says that pair programming is economical. Here are some findings.

In 1996, there was a report from Hill Air Force Base:

The two-person team approach places two engineers or two programmers in the same location (office, cubicle, etc.) with one workstation and one problem to solve. The team is not allowed to divide the task but produces the design, code, and documentation as if the team was a single individual. . . . Final project results were outstanding. Total productivity was 175 lines per person-month (lppm) compared to a documented average individual productivity of only 77 lppm. This result is especially striking when we consider two persons produced each line of source code. The error rate through software-system integration was three orders of magnitude lower than the organization's norm. Was the project a fluke? No. Why were the results so impressive? A brief list of observed phenomena includes focused energy, brainstorming, problem solving, continuous design and code walkthroughs, mentoring, and motivation. (Jensen 1996)

In 1998, Temple University Professor Nosek reported on his study of 15 full-time, experienced programmers working for 45 minutes on a challenging problem, important to their organization, in their own environment and with their own equipment. Five worked individually; ten worked collaboratively in five pairs. Conditions and materials used were the same for both the experimental (team) and control (individual) groups. This study provided statistically significant results, using a two-sided t-test. "To the surprise of the managers and participants, all the teams outperformed the individual programmers, enjoyed the problem-solving process more, and had greater confidence in their solutions." Combining their time, the pairs spent 60 percent more time on the task. However, because they worked in tandem, they were able to complete the task in less "wall-clock" time, in addition to producing better algorithms and code in less time. The majority of the programmers were initially skeptical of the value of collaboration in working on the same problem and thought it would not be an enjoyable process. However, results show collaboration improved both their performance and their enjoyment of the problem-solving process (Nosek 1998).

After reading these results, we decided to do an experiment of our own, one that ultimately produced groundbreaking results. In 1999 at the University of Utah, students in the Senior Software Engineering course participated in a structured experiment. The students were aware of the importance of the experiment, the need to keep accurate information, and the importance of each person (whether in the control group or the experimental group) to the outcome. All students attended the same classes, received the same instruction, and participated in class discussions on the pros and cons of pair programming. When asked on the first day of class, 35 of the 41 students (85 percent) indicated a preference for pair programming. (Later, many of that 85 percent admitted they were initially reluctant, but curious, about pair programming.) The students also understood that grades would be curved in separate pair/individual groupings, so that no one had to be concerned that the working arrangement would affect his or her final grade.

The students were divided into two groups; both groups were deliberately comprised of the same mix of high, average, and low performers. Thirteen students formed the control group in which all the students worked individually on all assignments. Twenty-eight students formed the experimental group in which all worked in two-person collaborative teams; collaboratively, they completed the same assignments as the individuals. (The collaborative pairs also did additional assignments to keep the overall workload the same between the two groups.) All 28 students in the experimental group had expressed an interest in pair programming, and some of the students in the control group had wanted to try pair programming. It is important to note that prior to enrolling in this class, students had had significant coding practice. Most students had had industry/internship experience and had written small compilers, operating system kernels, and interpreters in other classes.

Cycle time, productivity, and quality results were compared between the two groups. Students recorded information in a Web-based tool about the time they spent on each project. Quality was measured by the results of automated testing executed by an impartial teaching assistant.

As reported (Cockburn and Williams 2000; Williams et al. 2000; Williams 2000), our experimental class produced quantitative results supporting the pair programming results in industry. The students completed four assignments over a period of six weeks. Thirteen individuals and fourteen collaborative pairs completed each assignment. The pairs passed, on average, 15 percent more of the automated postdevelopment test cases (see Table 4.1). The difference in quality levels is statistically significant.

The pair results were also more consistent, while the individuals varied more about the mean. Individuals intermittently didn't hand in a program or handed it in late; pairs handed in their assignments on time. This result can be attributed to "Pair Pressure" as discussed in Chapter 3. The programmers admitted to working harder and smarter on programs because they did not want to let their partner down. Individuals did not have this form of pressure and did not perform as consistently.

Table 4-1 Percentage of Test Cases Passed

	Individuals	Collaborative Teams
Program 1	73.4%	86.4%
Program 2	78.1%	88.6%
Program 3	70.4%	87.1%
Program 4	78.1%	94.4%

Not only did pairs write programs that were of higher externally visible quality (for example, they passed more test cases), but their programs were consistently more than 20 percent shorter than their individual counterparts. Implementing functionality in fewer lines of code is commonly viewed as an indication of better design quality and lower projected maintenance costs (Boehm 1981). The individuals were more likely to produce "blob class" (Brown et al. 1998) designs—just to get the job done. The design from the pairs exploited more of the benefits of object-oriented programming. Their classes demonstrated more encapsulation and had more cohesive classes with better class-responsibility alignment. The individuals tended to have fewer classes that had many responsibilities, which would probably be more difficult to enhance and/or maintain.

Lots of nagging, low-severity software defects can become a big annoyance to customers. Even one high-severity software defect can come with a very high price tag for customers. William Malik, research director at Gartner, reports that 40 percent of all system crashes are software related. Hardware problems cause system outages of a few seconds to a few minutes, while software crashes typically bring down networks for several hours to several days. Some businesses, such as the New York Stock Exchange, can lose anywhere from $10,000 to several million dollars a minute when networks go down, which often happens due to software problems. Alan MacCormack, Harvard Business School professor, points out that systems are so complex now that they are impossible to test fully (Krantz and Iwata June 11, 2001). As a result, we must build quality into our products. Pair programming can help us do this.

The other piece of the economic equation is time. The gut reaction of many people is to reject the idea of pair programming because they assume there will be a 100 percent programmer-hour increase by putting two programmers on a job that one can do. If pair programming does, indeed, double the time, it certainly would be difficult to justify, even given the dramatic, expensive effects of poor quality just discussed. The University of Utah students recorded how much time they spent on their assignments via a Web-based data recording and information retrieval system. During an initial adjustment period in the first program (the "jelling" assignment, which took approximately ten hours), the pairs spent approximately 60 percent more person-hours to complete the program. Thereafter, the pairs spent on average only 15 percent more than the individuals, which was no longer statistically significant, because the average was driven up by two of the 13 pairs. The median amount of time spent by the individuals and the pairs was essentially identical. As a side note, the two pairs that spent the most time also spent the most time when they completed pre- and postexperiment programs individually. (Williams 2000; Cockburn and Williams 2000; Williams et al. 2000)

This still begs the question: Why would we ever invest an additional 15 percent on code development by introducing pair programming? The higher quality that is obtained in initial code development reduces future test and field support resource requirements. Typically, in systems tests it takes between one-half (Humphrey 1995) and two (Humphrey 1997) workdays to correct each defect. Industry data reports that between 33 and 88 hours are spent on each defect found in the field (Humphrey 1995). When each defect saved during code development can save defect correction time of between .5 and 88 hours, pair programming quickly becomes the cost-saving and time-saving alternative (Williams 2000). Appendix B demonstrates the overall life-cycle affordability of pair programming based on an in-depth economic analysis.

It should also be noted that if time-to-market/cycle time is a prime motivator for you, pair programming can get the job done in about half the time. Could the same thing be done with two programmers working independently? Not likely. Increased communication and training time would increase their total time, as Brooks has told us for over a quarter of a century with his "Brooks's Law" (1975). Additionally, the quality would not be as high.

Data with students is a start in convincing you about improvements using pair programming. But what about industrial studies? It is difficult to obtain statistically significant results from industry. We do offer two case studies, both received via personal communication to Laurie.

- Bill Wood and Bil Kleb of NASA Langley report that in 2001 a pair of programmers re-implemented a numerical algorithm for wave propagation that was originally developed in 1997. The individual programmer worked for 6 weeks to produce 2144 lines of code. The pair worked a total of 3 programmer weeks, implementing the same functionality in only 866 lines of code, comprised of 403 lines of production code and 463 lines of testing code. It is important to note that the individual did not write any testing code and that while the individual was very experienced in the language, the pair was learning a new language. By combining pair programming with extensive testing techniques, Wood and Kleb have much higher confidence in the new code.

- A technology company in India reports very impressive pair programming results. The prototype of a Voice-Over-IP project was done without pairing, although the actual project was done utilizing pair programming. The actual project was much more complex because it had to deal with meeting Quality of Service parameters, scalability, uptime, and so on. The paired project showed significant increases in productivity and quality. It is important to note that the manager for this project indicated that this project was a high-priority project. As a result, the teams worked nearly round the clock. The extremely high productivity numbers shown in Table 4-2 should not be considered as representative of pair programmers but rather should be considered in comparison to the solo programmers only. The data is summarized in Table 4-2.

Goal: I want to reduce my risk of losing a key person.

WIIFM: My stress level is reduced because I am not as concerned about the implications of losing a key person on the team and the resulting debilitation of my project. I feel more in control because key personnel cannot exercise their power by threatening to leave.

Table 4-2 India Technology Project Data

	Project One: Solo Programmers	Project Two: Pair Programmers
Project Size (KLOC)	20	520
Team Size	4	12
Effort (Person-Months)	4	72
Productivity (KLOC/Person-Month)	5	7.2
Productivity (KLOC/Pair-Month)	n/a	14.4
Unit Test Defects	107	183
	(5.34 defects/KLOC)	(0.4 defects/KLOC)
System Integration Defects	46	82
	(2.3 defects/KLOC)	(0.2 defects/KLOC)

Weinberg (1998) has a maxim, "If a programmer is indispensable, get rid of him as quickly as possible." His contention is that a project should not be a house of cards that collapses when a single "key" person is removed.

With pair programming, the project risk associated with losing this key programmer is reduced because there are multiple people familiar with each part of the system. If a pair works together consistently, then there are two people familiar with this particular area of the program. If the pairs rotate, many people can be familiar with each part. A common informal metric (invented by Jim Coplien) is referred to as the "truck number." "How many or few people would have to be hit by a truck (or quit) before the project is incapacitated?" The worst answer is "one." Having knowledge dispersed across the team increases the truck number and project safety.

We'll discuss the use of pair programming as a knowledge management technique more in Chapter 9.

Goal: I want my employees to be happy.

WIIFM: Undoubtedly, happier employees stay in their jobs longer. Turnover is very costly in both recruiting and training costs. Also, happier, less frustrated people are more positive about their jobs and are more eager to help the team meet the objectives.

The incorporation of pair programming has been shown to improve the engineers' job satisfaction and overall confidence while attaining the quality and cycle time results discussed earlier. Based on seven independent surveys of self-selected pair programmers, over 90 percent of pair programmers agreed that they enjoyed their jobs more when pair programming. The groups were also surveyed on whether working collaboratively made them feel more confident about their work. These results are even more positive—96 percent indicated that pair programming made them more confident.

Goal: I want to reduce the amount of time it takes to train a new person.

WIIFM: My training costs are reduced, which helps me manage my budget. New people can actually contribute to projects much earlier.

In *The Mythical Man Month* (1975), Brooks states his law: "Adding manpower to a late software project makes it later." He believes that communication costs are the major driver leading to this phenomenon. Brooks breaks these communication costs into training and intercommunication. Certainly, reducing training costs is a worthy objective.

Traditionally, people new to an organization are shown different parts of a system by senior staff personnel. This dedicated training time costs the senior personnel valuable hours. During these hours, neither the new person nor the trainer is making contributions toward the completion of the project. Through pair programming, the trainer teaches by *doing* (not showing), and direct contributions are actually made during the training time. Additionally, training seems to go much faster, and the new person learns the system more intimately.

We'll explore the beneftis of pair programming as a training technique further in Chapter 9.

Goal: I want my teams to work well together and to communicate more effectively and efficiently with each other.

WIIFM: My team works together better because they know each other and like each other. This makes them happier employees. It also greatly reduces information "islands" because people are more likely actually to talk to each other more often, sharing problems and solutions.

There are many stories of teams that started with pair programming. Before pair programming, people would walk into work in the morning at different times with a brown-bag lunch in their hands. They'd walk into their office or cubicle, put their lunch down and their headphones on. They'd tap, tap, tap on the keyboard all day. At some point, they'd take their lunch out of the brown bag and eat it. At the end of the day, they'd take off their headphones and head home. They would mainly communicate with other team members during meetings and via e-mail.

After pair programming, these teams were profoundly transformed. Pairing, the team members got to know each other better through the idle chitchat that goes on during pauses while pairing. A programmer might mention that he was going to a ball game or to her child's recital that night. The next day, whether they were pairing together, one might ask how the recital went or comment on the outcome of the game when meeting at the vending machine. As the team gets to know each other better, they are far more likely to talk with each other about both personal and technical matters. The communication barriers between each other start to crumble. Team members find each other much more approachable. They will struggle with questions or lack of information for less time before getting themselves out of their chair and going to ask the right person a question—because now they know that person quite well. The rapport and trust built between team members gives them the courage to ask each other for advice and guidance without feeling vulnerable and insufficient. Additionally, they feel better about their jobs because they know their teammates on a personal level.

We contend that communication is made more efficient in another important way. As we said earlier, Brooks considers training and intercommunication costs to be major cost factors. Brooks (1975) asserts that "if each part of the task must be separately coordinated with each other part, the [communication] effort increases as $n(n-1)/2$." It's easy to think about the items that need to be done in order to coordinate two interdependent parts: Dependencies need to be identified and scheduled accordingly, interfaces need to be specified, technical decisions might need to be made jointly, change management activities need to be accomplished, and so on. Additionally, progress might be slowed or completely halted if some critical coordination needs to occur when a team member is missing.

Let's think about how pair programming can make this communication more efficient. Consider first if a team does not rotate pairs but assigns larger pieces of functionality to static pairs. Instead of breaking the project into n parts, the project is broken into $(n/2)$ parts, and the communication effort increase is reduced from $n(n-1)/2$ to $n(n-2)/8$. When pairs work together, they make decisions on dependencies, technical aspects, and interfaces as they go. No separate coordination activities need to take place; no dependencies and interfaces need special documentation, improving the efficiency of team communication. If pairs do rotate, and programmers partner with the programmer with whom their task is interdependent, we believe this intercommunication cost can be even further reduced because needed communication about interfaces and other issues will happen during the natural course of pairing.

References

Boehm, B. (1981). *Software Engineering Economics*, Prentice Hall.

Brooks, F. P. (1995). *The Mythical Man Month: Anniversary Edition*, Addison-Wesley.

Brown, W. J., Malveau, R. C., McCormick, H. W., and Mowgray, T. J. (1998). *AntiPatterns*, Wiley Computer Publishing.

Cockburn, A. and Williams, L. (2000). "The Costs and Benefits of Pair Programming," *eXtreme Programming and Flexible Processes in Software Engineering—XP2000*, Cagliari, Sardinia, Italy.

Humphrey, W. S. (1995). *A Discipline for Software Engineering*, Addison-Wesley.

Humphrey, W. S. (1997). *Introduction to the Personal Software Process*, Addison-Wesley.

Jensen, R. W. (1996). "Management Impact on Software Cost and Schedule." *Crosstalk*, July, http://stsc.hill.af.mil/crosstalk/1996/jul/manageme.asp.

Krantz, M., and Iwata, E. (June 11, 2001). "Companies Bleed Cash when Computers Quit," *USA Today*, B1.

Nosek, J. T. (1998). "The Case for Collaborative Programming." *Communications of the ACM*, 105–108.

Weinberg, G. M. (1998). *The Psychology of Computer Programming, Silver Anniversary Edition*, Dorset House Publishing.

Williams, L. A. (2000). "The Collaborative Software Process," Ph.D. dissertation, University of Utah.

Williams, L., Kessler, R., Cunningham, W., and Jeffries, R. (2000). "Strengthening the Case for Pair-Programming." *IEEE Software*, July/August 2000, 19–25.

Gaining Support and Acceptance from Your Peers

You are not a manager, but from what you've heard and what you've read, you would like to try pair programming. What do you do now?

Mary Lynn Manns and Linda Rising have done a great deal of research on the introduction of new ideas into organizations. In *Introducing Patterns into Organizations* (2002), they define a pattern[1] language and observe the use of these patterns in small, medium, and large companies throughout the world. The recommendations in this chapter will be made in the context of pattern language. Each time we use a pattern from this pattern language, it will appear in **boldface;** the names of the patterns are quite intuitive.

If you are not a manager and are interested in trying pair programming within your organization, then according to Manns and Rising's pattern language, you are an **Evangelist**. You believe that pair programming will be valuable for your organization. You want to give it a shot and spread the word.

We suggest gradually introducing a very casual, noninvasive use of the practice with your peers. One thing to consider is that, as an industry, programmers are overcommitted. You probably are too. So launching the grassroots peer acceptance strategy requires a leap of faith on your part because you certainly don't want to give yourself any more work. So we encourage you to use a risk-mitigation strategy with yourself as well. Start small; you need to convince yourself that it's worthwhile before you can convince others. You also

---

[1] Patterns were inspired by architect Christopher Alexander (Alexander et. al 1977). A pattern is a problem that occurs over and over again in our environment and a description of the core of the solution to that problem. The core of this solution could be used a million times over without ever doing it the same way twice. A pattern language is a collection of patterns that build upon each other to generate a system.

don't want to work a lot of extra overtime because of your casual experimentation. By doing this, you **Test the Waters**.

Identify people on your team that seem especially interested in new ideas. Consider these folks as targeted **Innovators**. Manns and Rising advise, "[Innovators] are quick to see if something is worth their time, however, so they won't tolerate something half-baked. Make sure you've done your homework before enlisting their support." First, you can try to discuss pair programming nonchalantly with these folks over lunch or at the vending machine. Be sure to be prepared with a **Personal Touch**—in other words, a specific way that pair programming can personally help that person get his or her job done better. Rogers (1995) writes, "The relative advantage of an innovation . . . is positively related to its rate of adoption." One dimension of relative advantage is the savings an individual realizes in time and effort. Go back and reread Chapter 4. Your peers want to finish on time, with higher quality, and have more fun, don't they?

If you find someone else who is interested, that is wonderful. Quite often, programmers can find someone on their team willing to give it a try. Just start pairing for small bits of time together; make sure that you are both able to keep up with your assigned responsibilities so no one gets nervous. If you haven't found any receptive programmers, we suggest that you just start pairing with people on your team in small bits of time. In other words, **Just Do It**. Think about the makeup of your team. Who are you already friendly with? Who works in areas that you already understand pretty well? If you can think of a programmer or two who meets both of those criteria, they are great candidates to get started with.

You might see one of your candidates working. Pull up a chair next to him or her. If you've never discussed the subject before or that person hasn't been particularly receptive to the idea, don't say, "Want to try pair programming with me?" As we have said, many are resistant to trying pair programming. If you label what you're proposing, they might get anxious.

Just say, "Hey, what are you working on?" After you get an answer, say, "Could you help me for a bit?" Quite likely, the person will agree to give you some time; helping others boosts one's ego and reaffirms one's confidence. Work together for half an hour to a couple of hours, depending on when a natural break point occurs. Don't be too concerned about following the model of driver and navigator. At this point, say, "I think that went really well. You really helped me a lot—thanks. If you ever need help, be sure to ask. I'd be happy to return the favor." Repeat this process a few more times. We feel quite sure that if you start to try pairing with a peer, most often it will work out. If not, don't get discouraged; try it with someone else. When you feel that you have established a mutually beneficial pair programming relationship with someone, you should explicitly discuss the experiences with that person and let him or her know that what you have been doing is pair programming (if it hasn't been figured out yet). Assuming the person agrees it was beneficial, a pair programming relationship is born!

Once each of you firmly feels that pair programming is helpful, look around your team for other candidates to work with for small chunks of time. If each of you starts to pair with one other, then four on your team are casually experimenting with the technique. In this way, the team of **Innovators** will gradually grow to the **Early Majority**. Ultimately, this can lead to a **Grass Roots** effort whereby there are enough **Innovators** to provide a foundation of pair programming within the organization, and the practice can naturally be diffused to others.

Assuming that you are all getting your work done on schedule, it's probably not necessary to get your manager officially involved until there is acceptance among a handful or more of the team members. If you are satisfied with how things are going and don't want to take it to the next level where more widespread pair programming is part of your team dynamic, then just keep on doing what you are doing. The majority of the managers won't be concerned if they see their programmers working together from time to time. However, we encourage you always to consider taking it to the next level as time goes on. For one thing, pair programming might fizzle over time if pairing and the rotation of the pairs are not ingrained into the practices of your team. When you ask a peer to help you, you might get a reply too often that he or she is busy.

Once you do feel as if it would be advantageous to spread the practice around the team and to increase the use, it is time to talk to your manager. You need to enlist him or her as a **Local Leader.** "Site leadership is critical. . . . Experience suggests that where the technology will really make an impact across a broad spectrum, versus just a small project, is in those cases where [local] management . . . takes responsibility for committing the site to the technology" (Korson and Vaishnavi 1996). If you have any informal metrics about the pairing work that has already been done, gather them together. Can you say that tasks have been done any faster? Can you get any test or field results that show quality is improving? Do you have any stories about how much you have learned, how many bugs got caught early by your partner, how the team is communicating better, and so on? How many on the team have tried it and liked it, not tried it, or tried it and not liked it? Maybe it's time to go back, reread Chapter 4, and prepare a convincing case (**Pieces of Clay**) for the good of the team.

Propose to your manager that you run a **Brown Bag** lunch or a department meeting (**Do Food)** to increase involvement where information about pair programming can be shared. At this meeting, have one (or some) of the **Innovators** informally give a **Hometown Story** in which he or she shares a particular pair programming experience. It is best if these individuals are known and respected within the team, a **Respected Techie**. Rogers (1995) has shown that "the trail of a new idea by a peer like themselves can substitute, at least in part, for [an individual's] own trial."

Appendix A outlines a half-day session that can be run with members of your team.

References

Manns, M. L. and Rising, L. (2002). *Introducing Patterns into Organizations*, Addison-Wesley.

Korson, T. D. and Vaishnavi, V. K. (1996). *Object Technology Centers of Excellence*, Manning Publication Co.

Rogers, E. M. (1995). *Diffusion of Innovations*, 4th ed., The Free Press.

Transitioning to Pair Programming by Choice

We start this chapter with a true story about a presentation Laurie did to introduce an organization to pair programming. She's done quite a few of these pair programming presentations and figured she knew how the day would go. She hooked her laptop to the projector and people started to file in slowly. Usually before a presentation officially starts, people casually chat with Laurie about their experiences trying pair programming, or they comment on a paper they read. Funny thing, though, no one talked to her this day. The vice president of software development, Danny (named changed), walked in and introduced himself to Laurie and Laurie started the presentation. Because she'd done this presentation many times, she knew when questions would start flowing or when people would generally laugh. Nothing; There was no reaction at all to what she was saying. She thought this was kind of odd and started *really* looking at her audience's faces. They looked like they were at a funeral. It was tough to get through the rest of the talk. The only one who asked any questions or made any comments was Danny, and oh, yes, there was one woman (we'll call her Kimberly) in the back of the room, bless her heart. She smiled and nodded at Laurie the whole time. Thank goodness for Kimberly. After the talk, Laurie did a "Pair Programming Readiness" survey that she has often done. The survey assesses the team's perception of how helpful pair programming will be and what specific concerns they might have. After taking the survey, the employees silently filed out of the room.

After the talk, Laurie met up with Kimberly in the hallway. She was still smiling. She said, "I really, really enjoyed your talk. I am so happy you came to talk to us. I can't wait to get started pair programming."

Laurie then met with the man who arranged her trip. He said he was going to see who wanted to go to lunch with her, and Laurie should wait in the lobby. After what seemed like an hour, he emerged with his two best friends (probably the only ones he could arm wrestle into coming to lunch). When they sat down for lunch, Laurie popped the question: "Danny is forcing you guys to pair program, isn't he?" All of them stared in disbelief that it was so obvious and shook their heads to agree. The three then admitted that Danny had read some papers Laurie and Bob Kesler had published about pair programming (Williams and Kessler 2000; Williams et al. 2000). When he was done reading, he said to himself, "That's it! We're doing it." He asked someone who worked for him to contact Laurie and bring her to talk to his group. Meanwhile, he made some form of proclamation to his team, "Read these articles. We're going to start pair programming. Laurie Williams is going to come talk to us about the practice, and then we'll get started after she leaves."

After lunch, Laurie went to the airport and started flipping through the "Pair Programming Readiness" surveys. The message was clear, "If you make us pair program, we're all quitting." Needless to say, this organization never started pair programming (poor Kimberly).

That experience inspired the writing of this chapter. We aim to help you avoid this kind of situation. First, we will discuss some wonderful work on the successful diffusion of innovation in software development organizations done by Gina Green and Alan Hevner (1999; 2000). Then we'll give you some advice on how to proceed cautiously if you are a manager who is tempted to force your employees to pair. Finally, we'll address the programmer who has already been or is currently being forced to pair.

Green and Hevner's Findings

"Several promising new tools and techniques have improved software development, but most are either not widely adopted or often quickly abandoned" (Green and Hevner 2000). Green and Hevner's report focuses on why this often happens and how we can prevent it from happening. We hope their advice can ease the diffusion of pair programming through an organization, particularly when initiated by management. We aim for sustained use of pair programming rather than abandonment of this new technique.

Green and Hevner developed a research model of diffusion of software development techniques. The two researchers developed the research model including twelve research hypotheses. Using surveys, they then evaluated their model by performing an extensive field study of industrial software developers. The model and subsequent field study showed that developer involvement in the implementation process and the characteristics of the environment into which the techniques are introduced are key factors in the diffusion success. Specifically, their research demonstrated that developers are more satisfied with using software development innovations if

- **they have *increased* choice in when to use that innovation.** This suggests that managers should provide to individual developers as much freedom as possible to decide when to apply innovative software development techniques, such as pair programming.

- **they have *decreased* process control in how to use that innovation.** The findings of the study indicate that in a complex task environment, such as software development, decreases in personal control can result in greater satisfaction. This was a particularly interesting finding that would discourage an "if you want to pair, go ahead and pair—I don't care" arrangement and encourage a more organized approach of pairing and possibly the rotation of pairs, still giving the employees the freedom to choose when to pair and what to do when they pair. Likewise it is not advisable for the manager to say, "Now that you understand the theory of pair programming, I will let each of your teams decide how best to practice it." This gives the developers too much process control leading to confusion on how best to implement the technique and the risk of different teams using disparate, and maybe conflicting, pair programming techniques. Thus the manager thinks he is giving the developers desired flexibility; instead, he is creating a confusing environment for practicing the technique. Some level of consistent organizational standards and procedures for implementing pair programming is essential.

- **their manager encouraged them to use the innovative technique.** Again this would discourage an "if you want to pair, go ahead and pair—I don't care" attitude on the part of management. The employees need to know their manager is supportive of pairing and that "we pair program in this department." To be most effective, managers need to find how far they can go with encouragement without crossing the "forcing" line.

- **the innovation increases the predictability of their work.** As we said in Chapter 4, the pairs in the pair programming study at the University of Utah performed more consistently and predictably than individuals. Not only did they achieve higher scores, but the standard deviation of their scores was much lower than that of individuals. Pair pressure causes us to "rise to the occasion" and perform. Therefore, according to these findings, programmers should appreciate the added predictability of their results while pairing.

The two researchers also support the assertions of Moore and Benbasat (1991) that *mandating* the use of a new technique is not good. Instead, managers should *encourage* the use of the new technique to create a situation of voluntary use.

Advice for Management

Undoubtedly, Danny's technique of mandating pair programming is not advisable—his behavior could be a supportive example for Green and Hevner. Most often, change cannot be "managed" from the top.

> Harvard's John Kotter, in a study of 100 top management-driven "corporate transformation" efforts, concluded that more than half did not survive the initial phases. He found a few that were "very successful" and a few that were "utter failures." The vast majority lay "somewhere in between, with a distinct tilt toward the lower end of the scale. . . ." This failure to sustain significant change recurs again and again despite substantial resources committed to the change effort (many are bankrolled by top management), talented and committed people "driving the change," and high stakes. (Senge et al. 1999)

We have some advice for managers who would like to intoduce pair programming in their organization. Again, as in Chapter 5, we frame this recommendation in Manns and Rising's (2002) pattern language for introducing innovation into an organization. Again the patterns that we use are in **boldface**. We assume you are the **Local Leader,** but in this situation you can also become the **Evangelist** by putting your managerial authority second when it comes to the diffusion of pair programming.

1. Ask an open-minded, respected senior programmer, a **Respected Techie**, to read about pair programming. This person should actually try the technique several times by wandering into team member's offices. By finding an opportunity to **Just Do It**, he or she can use the techniques outlined in Chapter 5 for working with others and can also use the pattern when training new personnel. Do not rush this step. It is very important for the senior person genuinely to be convinced of the technique through actual experiences, not just by reading about them. If this person does not attain this level of appreciation for the technique, ask him or her not to criticize pair programming publicly; pick another senior developer. (Remember, we already know that pair programming is not for all.)

2. Once a senior developer is genuinely convinced of the technique, encourage him or her to gain the support of other programmers, some **Innovators**, by continuing to use the suggestions in Chapter 5. Additionally, you can ask the senior developer to organize a Pair Programming Tutorial. Appendix A outlines a half-day session which can be run with members of the team.

3. Once there is support for the technique among a few developers and enough **Early Adopters**, it is time for an educational session for a larger organization. This session should be run by the senior developer, preferably without any management present. It could be a **Brown Bag** lunch or a department meeting (**Do Food**). The other programmers who have tried and like the technique should be encouraged to share their experiences by discussing a **Hometown Story**.

   The **Early Adopters** should be prepared with a **Personal Touch**—in other words, a specific way that pair programming can personally help each person get his or her job done better. Also be prepared for negative reaction and skeptics (**Fear Less**). It is a big change, one that many would likely fear before trying. "In presentations, bring up the negative things you have heard or anticipate what your detractors might say. If you don't bring these issues up, you are more vulnerable when someone else raises them.

This approach of inviting resistance makes sure that all concerns are heard" (Manns and Rising 2002).

4. During this educational session, several things should be accomplished:

- Programmers who are interested in trying the technique should sign up. Using this information, the team should develop an informal plan for who should try pairing with whom.

- The initial trial of the technique should feel low risk for all involved: **Test the Waters**. Most will still be concerned that, for them, pairing will double their workload. Initial trials could be in short intervals of one to two hours. Some organizations have, instead, chosen small groups of volunteers as their designated experimenters. These developers have paired full time for four to six weeks and report results back to the larger group.

- Put in place a system of feeding back concerns and successes of these trials. This system can be as informal as stopping in the senior programmer's office periodically or as formal as keeping track of progress/defects. This is the **Evaluation Phase.**

- The team should then discuss what would convince them that pair programming is or is not a valid technique. The team should decide what data they want to collect and how long it will take for them to decide on the validity of the technique.

- The team should discuss organizational guidelines for use of the pair programming and some success criteria. For example, some organizations have policies such as pairing takes place between 9:00–11:00 and 1:00–3:00, no meetings should be held during this time, interruptions of any kind should be avoided.

5. **Involve Everyone.** A strategy for reaching everyone, including skeptics, is to pair an avid **Early Adopter** with a skeptic (**Adopt a Skeptic**).

Once the official trial has completed, evaluate the results, and democratically determine the future of pair programming in your organization. If it is to be fairly widespread, you'll need to read Part Two, which will help you with some implementation items.

Managers must also have a consistent message for the employees. If managers encourage pair programming and then continue to value the heroics of individuals, the team will have a very hard time with pair programming. Widespread use of pair programming involves a cultural shift in the values of the organization—away from individual and toward team recognition and goals. The manager must carefully think through the implications to his or her own reward structure and to that of the larger organization, beyond the team itself.

Never forget: Mandating is bad; structuring, encouraging, and supporting are good.

Advice for Programmers

Perhaps, unfortunately, you have a manager like Danny. Now what? We advise you to hold off on quitting your job; give pair programming a fair chance. There are some things about pairing that could really help you, if you will just give it a try.

Even if everyone else is saying it, we advise you not to make any public statements such as "If I have to pair program, I'm quitting." Once you make a statement like that, it is hard to go back on your word and to give pair programming a fair try because you may feel like a traitor in the eyes of your "anti-pair programming" peers.

Suspend disbelief. Jim and Michele McCarthy (2002) recommend that their teamwork training classes *pretend* to have a shared vision. Pretend pair programming will work so that you will give it a fair shot. All in all, we encourage you not to form an opinion until after you have tried pair programming for a couple of weeks. Others have found that it could take a couple of weeks and a few horrible pairing sessions until they get into the flow of pair programming. If your manager sees you giving it a fair try and you still don't like it after a couple of weeks, he or she should accept the fact that maybe you don't work better in a pair. The manager needs to appreciate the contributions of solo programmers and to be reminded that, in our experience, not everyone works best as a pair programmer.

References

Green, G. and Hevner, A. R. (1999). "Perceived Control of Software Developers and Its Impact on the Successful Diffusion of Information Technology," *Carnegie Mellon Special Report*, CMU/SEI-98-SR-013.

Green, G. and Hevner, A. R. (2000). "The Successful Diffusion of Innovations: Guidance for Software Development Organizations," *IEEE Software*, vol. 17, November/December 2000, pp. 96–103.

Manns, M. L. and Rising, L. (2003). *Introducing Patterns into Organizations*, Addison-Wesley, in press.

McCarthy, J. and McCarthy, M. (2002). *Software for Your Head: Core Protocols for Creating and Maintaining Shared Vision*, Addison-Wesley.

Moore, G. and Benbasat, I. (1991). "Development of an Instrument to Measure the Perceptions of Adopting an Information Technology Innovation," *Information Systems Research*, vol. 2, September 1991, pp. 192–222.

Senge, P., Kleiner, A., Roberts, C., Ross, R., Roth, G., Smith, B. (1999). *The Dance of Change: The Challenges to Sustaining Momentum in Learning*, Doubleday.

Williams, L. A. and Kessler, R. R. (2000). "All I Ever Needed to Know About Pair Programming I Learned in Kindergarten," in *Communications of the ACM*, vol. 43, May 2000.

Williams, L. A., Kessler, R., Cunningham, W., and Jeffries, R. (2000). "Strengthening the Case for Pair-Programming," in *IEEE Software*, July/August 2000, pp. 19–25.

Problem, Problems

It would be great if everything about pair programming was sunshine and roses, a miracle cure for all your ills. However, there are some cautions we need to share so your pair programming experience can be as effective as possible. (Many of these were provided to us by Andrew McKinlay of Suneido Software.)

Dependency

Once you start to pair, you really grow to like it; it makes you feel a bit uneasy to program alone. One of Laurie's earliest pair programming students said, "When I program alone, I feel like I lost half my brain." In *Extreme Programming Applied: Programming to Win* (Auer 2001), Ken Auer describes a scenario where a costly error was introduced while his partner was in the restroom!

So what do you do if the right partner is not available? Freeze? Decide to check your e-mail and surf the Web until he or she is available? Of course not! First, consider if there's another part of the system you can work on in which you can find a partner. Next think if there's anyone you can help by pairing with that person. But in the end, we've programmed alone before; we can do it again! Just proceed a bit more cautiously (since you're working alone), and make sure to review your work with your partner when you are able to get back together.

Scheduling

Without pairing, scheduling everyone's time is easier. "You do the proxy agent and report back here on the 19th." Actually, if everyone works with the same person all the time, scheduling is not any harder. "You two do the proxy agent and report back here on the 10th."

Scheduling becomes more of a conflict if who pairs with whom is changed regularly. Every team member will own different aspects of the system and will "recruit" the right partner depending on what he or she is doing. This can create situations where a person might want to clone himself or herself (at least once). Who does what when? There are many benefits to this pair rotation, so we don't want to make the scheduling/logistical issues sound insurmountable, but it does need to be dealt with. We discuss these benefits and some scheduling arrangements in Chapter 9.

The Ever-Popular Expert

This is a continuation of the scheduling problem. Within the team, experts—the GUI expert, the database expert, the kernel expert—emerge. Everybody wants to pair with these folks when the task "touches" the GUI, the database, or the kernel.

Ultimately, the experts and the heroes need to have time to work on the tasks they own themselves (the GUI, the database, and the kernel). You need to ensure that whatever scheduling algorithm you choose allows the expert time to do his or her own thing, using other teammates as partners.

An experienced pair programmer shares some advice:

If there is some number of designated pairing periods during the day, let the experts spend (for example) at least half on their own tasks. On one project, where the experts were in extremely heavy demand, we did this the other way around: Experts had designated "office hours" and could be used as consultants only on that schedule and only by "signing up" for their time in advance.

Colocation

Pairing means that partners must be sitting side-by-side, in the same location, at the same time. What if Danny and Chris need to pair, but Chris likes to get in very early to beat the traffic and Danny gets in much later because he has to drive his kids to school? Or perhaps, Kimberly's gotten used to working from home a few days a week or does so whenever her school-age kids are sick? Does introducing pair programming mean the freedoms these programmers have come to enjoy are taken away? If so, maybe they'll find another job that allows them these freedoms.

This is a sensitive and tricky issue. The resolution requires balance: balance between the needs of the project and the needs of the employees. We don't have all the answers, but we can offer a few ideas. First, to accommodate the freedoms of flex hours, consider having reasonable "core pair programming hours." All employees should be in work and available for pairing during those hours. During the noncore hours, programmers can do things that are typically done alone,—like answering e-mails, writing documentation, learning new tools, researching new techniques, and so on.

For the "work from home" crew or for the growing numbers of geographically distributed teams, you can consider distributed pair programming. This is becoming increasingly popular. We discuss it more in Chapter 26. We won't say that distributed pair programming is as effective as colocated pair programming, but it can be a valid option, particularly when the alternative is solo programming.

Noise and Facility Considerations

Effective pairs chatter; silence is a danger signal for a dysfunctional pair. This is not as much of a problem for other pairs as it is for the soloists who are trying to work near the pairs. Resolving this problem may require a commitment from the organization in terms of a facility change or equipment purchase. Pairing can also be difficult if cubicles or desks are arranged improperly. Turn to Chapter 8 to read about this and other facility considerations.

Concentration

Some people feel that they cannot achieve the same level of concentration and creativity when they work with a partner. In the November/December 2001 issue of *IEEE Software*, Robert Glass writes:

Many of us prefer to work for a burst of creative time in isolation, getting back together with our team when we have pieces of information to share and decisions to make. I cannot imagine holding ongoing conversations with a pairmate when I am operating in creative mode.

We acknowledge that there are many different personality types and modes of working effectively. Laurie's advice to Robert (in a letter to the editor) and to others who feel this way is to work alone if you feel you need to in order to be most creative. Investigate something, make a little prototype, but be open to revising your brainstormed-in-isolation solution when you get back with your partner. Most certainly, your partner can think of something you didn't think of when you were alone.

Disagreements

Disagreements happen. Following are some strategies for resolving conflicts:

- Each of you go off alone for a specified period of time to cool off and to investigate what you feel so strongly about. During this time, you might convince yourself that you are "oh-so-right," or you might find there are problems with your approach. Get back and report your results to your partner. Try again at coming up with a joint solution. If you really can't come to a resolution, consult a team coach/leader or other person of expertise.
- Do a CRC card (Bellin and Simone 1997) session. This gets you away from the computer and might involve other people besides just the two of you.
- Take a walk around the building—together!

Most important, have the conviction not to compromise when you believe it is not prudent. We want to avoid the "worst of both worlds" solutions in order to resolve a conflict.

Overconfidence

There may be a feeling that a pair can do no wrong. If you're working together, you might convince yourself that whatever you do together must be right. Remain cautious and careful! Especially if your organization does not do reviews, the pair must consistently maintain a quality focus.

Detailed testing can lessen the danger of overconfidence. See Appendix D for a discussion on testing.

Rushing

In Chapter 3, we discussed pair pressure and how focused a pair can become in order to finish the task at hand before they need to separate. We claimed that this leads to time efficiencies because "work expands to fill all available time." However, we must also caution pairs not to rush to complete something and do a poor job in the process. If a task must roll over to another pairing session, the task must roll over to another pairing session! Slow down, and do it right together.

Skill Imbalances

Skill imbalances can be tough to stomach. A team member should ideally realize that bringing up the skill level of a weaker team member is beneficial for the team as a whole. However, we know not all people have this type of patient, endearing personality. New folks should specifically be paired with mentoring types, lest they feel unwelcome or frustrated in the hands of a partner who wants to make only personal progress. This mentor must also give up control and allow the less skilled team member to drive most of the time. When the mentor is directing most of the activity, it's better for the trainee to be typing and not just listening. The student might not be assertive enough to ask for the keyboard. Mentors, watch out for an overly passive student; this could be a sign you're going too fast!

Probably more frustrating is a partner with a weaker skill level who has no desire to improve or who has a poor work ethic. On the one hand, we must remember that not all people have the personal motivation to be an "A player," and we need to respect a myriad of people. On the other hand, team members who are downright slack need to be removed from the team.

Working with a partner gives us added confidence that what we are creating is correct. Naturally, we should feel more confident with a strong partner and feel more cautious (that we need to consider taking more personal responsibility) with a weaker, inexperienced partner.

There are also skill imbalances in typing. A very experienced person might just be a slow typist. This, too, can be frustrating and requires patience.

Chapters 13 and 14 give more advice about skill imbalances.

Simply Not for All

As we've said before, not everyone can pair or will want to pair. Pairing might not work for someone who is too introverted, soft-spoken, or lacks confidence. Perhaps this person can "grow out" of that with a nonthreatening pairing with a fabulous mentor or with another introverted, soft-spoken person. Pairing might also not work because someone is too self-centered or too egotistical or because he or she feels threatened—threatened to expose weaknesses in his or her knowledge or threatened to produce or lose his or her job. If you feel like you can't pair, do some self-examination to see if you can enlarge your comfort zone to include pairing.

We must, however, continue to respect the work of pairs and soloists.

Summary: Maintenance Required

Casual pairing needs no maintenance. If someone wants help, he or she can hopefully recruit someone to pair with for a while. No long-term relationship or arrangement is needed.

For more widespread pairing, there needs to be support and encouragement from the team coach/leader and the manager lest pairing will fade over time. After 20 or more years of studies supporting code inspections as an effective and efficient means of defect removal, most programmers avoid inspections like the plague. Pair programming doesn't have 20 years of studies. Programmers might still hang on to the belief they can do it faster if they worked alone. This might cause them to avoid pairing when they're in a time crunch. Collect and disseminate information/metrics to the team on the effeciveness of pairing. Do spot checks to make sure people are really pairing and are pairing effectively. This is a perfect application for Management by Walking Around (also commonly known as MBWA). Are people pairing? Are the pairs talking to each other? Are the roles of driver and navigator being rotated?

And, as we suggested, revised scheduling procedures and facilities will be needed.

Carefully consider the issues of this chapter. Go into pair programming with your eyes open.

References

Auer, K. and Miller, R. (2002). *Extreme Programming Applied: Playing to Win,* Addison-Wesley.

Bellin, D. and Simone, S. (1997). *The CRC Card Book*, Addison-Wesley.

Glass, Robert (2001), "Extreme Programming: The Good, the Bad, and the Bottom Line," *IEEE Software,* Vol. 18, No. 6, pp. 111–112.

Getting Started with Pair Programming

In order to implement pair programming beyond casual use, there are some issues to consider. We will discuss them in Part Two. In Chapter 8 we discuss some facility changes you may need to make so that pairs can work effectively and comfortably together. In Chapter 9 we discuss pair rotation within the team and its several beneficial aspects, including enhancing team spirit and communication. Additionally, pair rotation can be used to facilitate knowledge management and as a training technique. In Chapter 10 we discuss several other items to consider as you move toward pair programming. Finally, in Chapter 11, we will share some tips and tricks of effective pair programmers.

Workplace Layout

There are some important ergonomic considerations for pair programmers. In this chapter we will discuss some basic workplace needs to facilitate the sharing between pair programmers. Hopefully these needs can be accomplished without spending any money. Then we discuss some alternate arrangements, which can further enhance the effectiveness and satisfaction of the pairs.

The Basic Needs

As a bare minimum, the two pair programmers need to be able to sit comfortably side by side with a fairly large (17-inch minimum) monitor between them. The driver should be sitting squarely in front of the keyboard and mouse. The navigator must have a clear view of the display. When the driver and navigator switch roles, it should simply mean that the keyboard and mouse slide from one person to the other. A danger signal is when the two are tempted to get up and swap chairs when they switch roles. If this is the case, then the navigator probably does not have a decent viewing/contributing position. It is far less than ideal for the navigator to be sitting directly behind the driver, "breathing down the driver's neck."

These basic layout specifications can probably be accomplished in most workplaces without any expenditure as long as there are straight tables available. We have found that two programmers can comfortably sit side by side at a six-by-three foot table. Many report that convex tables (with an outer curve) work very well because the programmers don't need to worry about bumping chairs. Some cubicles are arranged so that the computer is located in the corner with cabinets on either side. This arrangement would need to be changed for effective pairing; very small tables are equally poor.

A programmer would pair with another by 'visiting' the workplace of his or her partner. Code would be accessible to their workstation via a network.

Some Suggested Workplace Enhancements

Experienced pairs have done many things to enhance their workplace arrangements. Although these alternatives generally require some capital expenditures, we are fortunate today that computers are very affordable, making some of thefollowing suggestions feasible.

- **Cave and Commons:** "The best environment I can think of is small cubbies (like study carrels) around the periphery of the room, because people need privacy to take calls from their proctologist. In the middle of the room are tables set up for pairing. The cubbies might or might not have computers, but the hottest machines are always in the middle. I have imagined that the cubbies are offices with doors, but really small" (Wiki 2001, contributed by Kent Beck).

  With this arrangement, developers do not take ownership of any of the common workstations and can dynamically share a dual workstation in the common area. Understandably, many programmers do not want to give up the right to own some of their own turf and have only shared space. In many cases, they have earned their own cubicle or office and do not want to give it up. The "caves"—small offices with doors or a shared cubicle with assigned desks (as are common today)—provide programmers with a home base where they can keep their belongings and have some privacy.

- **One Computer, Two Displays, Two Keyboards, Two Mice:** Many pair programmers very much prefer for each member of a pair to have his or her own display, keyboard, and mouse, all attached to one computer.

  This can easily be accomplished by utilizing the USB port and a dual video card; or, alternatively, keyboard and mouse switches and two video cards. Also, consider wireless keyboards and mice. It is great if each programmer can have his or her own, which can be brought to the pairing sessions.

Those who have this kind of setup believe that each member is alert and engaged and that control can more easily pass between the driver and the navigator. The navigator can very easily and momentarily take control and say, "What if we do this?"

Bil Kleb and Bill Wood at NASA Langley use their two displays in another way—as a virtual, ultrawide desktop. This approach better accomodates the screen real estate necessary for the test-first programming style they practice.[1] One screen displays the automated unit testing code while the other displays the corresponding production code. This allows a fluid exchange between driving and navigating for both the test code and the production code.

- **Laptops:** Each programmer can have a laptop. They can work on their laptop in their own "caves" and bring it to pairing sessions. This arrangement requires only that the laptops can connect to the network in either place. In this case, a wireless network would improve the ease with which parings can occur.

Interpair Communications

Effective communication, both within a pair and with other pairs, is paramount. Without much effort, programmers need to see each other, ask each other questions, and make decisions on things such as integration issues, lest these questions/issues are not discussed adequately. Programmers also benefit from "accidentally" overhearing other conversations to which they can have vital contributions. Separate offices and cubicles can inhibit this necessary exchange. "If any one thing proves that psychological research has been ignored by working managers, it's the continuing use of half partitions to divide workspace into cubicles. . . . Like many kings, some managers use divide-and-conquer tactics to rule their subjects, but programmers need contact with other programmers" (Weinberg 1998).

RoleModel Software, located in Holly Springs, North Carolina, has created the eXtreme Programming Software Studio. Their workstation layout supports both intra- and interpair communication. Tables are arranged as shown in Figure 8.1.

---

[1] Ultimately Bil and Bill chose a single wide-screen display (at least 2,000 horizontal pixels).

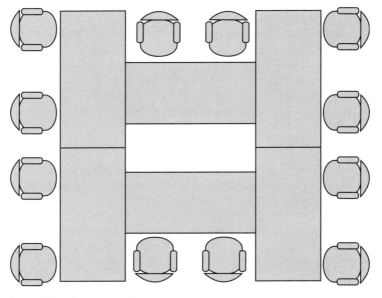

Figure 8-1 RoleModel Software Workstation Layout

One pair sits at each of these six tables; the pair can certainly communicate. However, with this layout, pairs can very easily communicate and "overhear" what is going on with the pairs to either side of or across from them. They can also interact with the other pairs fairly easily.

Development Environments

As with keyboard and mouse preferences, many developers have strong development environment (Visual SlickEdit, Visual Cafe, VisualAge) and debugger preferences. Ideally, there is a standardized environment. If not, then forcing one to change his or her environment might be enough to turn someone sour on pairing. In XP Applied (Auer and Miller 2002), Auer and Miller suggest, "in order to broaden their horizons, people must agree to program in a different environment for at least half the time for the next n weeks. n won't have to be too high before they decide they can converge on a single environment."

Noise Considerations

We have observed that effective pair programmers communicate with each other at least once every minute. Compared to the days when everyone worked alone, the workplace will be considerably nosier with pairing. Most pairs have said that they are so intent on their work, they can easily block out the noise. Some say it takes a few weeks to learn to block out the noise, which is another good reason to try pairing for a few weeks before making a decision on whether you prefer it over solo programming.

Others have a very delicate attention span. These folks may genuinely do better working alone in a quiet environment.

Those who work well in pairs can block out the noise of other pairs. However, their solo programming neighbors must be considered. There needs to be a sufficient barrier between pairing programmers and solo programmers to prevent disrupting the solo programmer. Preferably the groups should be separated by a door or at least by a tall (72") partition. Alternatively, a white noise machine can be installed to mask the murmur of the pairs. Studies have shown (DeMarco and Lister 1987) that [solo] programmers who worked in a quiet workplace were one third more likely to deliver zero-defect work. So, the impact of pair noise on solo programmers must be carefully considered.

One Last Thing

The navigator should not point on the screen with a finger. You know how we programmers hate paw prints on our displays! Use a stylus instead.

References

Auer, K. and Miller, R. (2002), *Extreme Program Applied*; *Playing to Win*, Addison-Wesley.

Weinberg, G. M. (1998). *The Psychology of Computer Programming, Silver Anniversary Edition*, Dorset House Publishing.

Wiki (2001). "Pair Programming Ergonomics," in Portland Pattern Repository, http://c2.com/cgi/wiki?PairProgrammingErgonomics.

Pair Rotation: Communication, Knowledge Management, and Training

Let's say you have a ten-person software development team, and you want to use pair programming. One way of implementing it would be to pair everyone and have five pairs that would work together. We believe a preferred way of implementing pair programming would be to have the pairs switch partners periodically. The advantages of rotating are that the programmers learn more about the whole product by pairing with different people: they team with the person who can help them the most on a particular task, and communication increases significantly. Also, you don't have to worry as much about pairs becoming dysfunctional and the need to switch around all the pairs because two particular people just can't get along. The two people who don't get along can probably stand to work together in half-day or full-day increments.

In this chapter, we'll describe a pair rotation strategy and how many companies determine who pairs with whom and for how long. Then we'll talk about the knowledge management, training, and communication advantages of pair rotation.

Pairing with the Right Partner

When people hear about rotating pairs, they often have the vision that this creates lots of jack-of-all-trades, masters-of-none generalists and discourages specialization. This section gives a simplified example of how to maintain specialists, spread knowledge around the team, and still enjoy the other benefits of pair programming. The example may seem rigid and prescribed. In actuality, pair rotation often occurs very casually without any formal schedule because team members learn how to maximize the benefits of pairing by choosing the right partner for the right situation. Also note that in a training scenario, it is best if the new person rotates around the group a bit, pairing with patient, mentoring types within the team, until he or she is assigned an area of specialty.

Consider a simple drink vending machine program. This program logically divides into four pieces: the GUI, the customer capabilities logic, the machine maintenance logic, and the data structures to run the whole program. Based on each employee's previous experience and expertise, he or she is assigned one of the following four pieces:

Team Member	Responsibility
Christopher	GUI
Brian	Customer Capabilities
Kimberly	Machine Maintenance
Chelsea	Data Structures

Based on what these individuals are working on during any given day, they have a logical partner in the team member who has the expertise and/or owns the functionality most closely related to the task at hand. For example, consider the following pairings:

Task	Task Owner	Partner
GUI for "Buy Drink"	Christopher	Brian
GUI for "Add Inventory"	Christopher	Kimberly
GUI for "Add Recipe"	Christopher	Kimberly
Input Coins/Return Coins	Brian	Christopher
Select Drink	Brian	Chelsea
Ingredient Data Structure	Chelsea	Kimberly
Recipe Data Structure	Chelsea	Kimberly
Add Ingredients	Kimberly	Chelsea
Customer Analysis	Kimberly	Christopher

As the GUI expert, Christopher is the owner of every GUI task. His partner is the person whose code the GUI is "touching." By pairing, Christopher gains the continual reviewer, brainstorming partner. However, his partner is also there to share expertise on the inner workings of the program logic that his GUI interacts with. His partner also gains great insight on the GUI it needs to interact with. In turn, Christopher will then partner with Brian and Kimberly when they work on their program logic for customer capabilities and machine maintenance. Brian and Kimberly will then own the task and Christopher will be the partner. All gain knowledge on how best to have their respective code interact while maintaining their area of specialty. All gain by having the expert in the area their code "touches" sitting right by their sides. All broaden their project knowledge.

You will notice that Christopher (GUI) and Chelsea (data structures) never pair and that Kimberly (machine maintenance) and Brian (customer capabilities) never pair. This is because their code does not interact directly with each other, so they are not "logical" partners. If their code does interact in any way, they should pair with each other for those tasks. Alternatively, Christopher/Chelsea and Kimberly/Brian may pair specifically for the purpose of broadening their project knowledge.

Partner Assigning Logistics

So how do these dynamic pairings get assigned? We will describe two very different ways; many variations occur. There is one common denominator, though. In order for pair rotation to occur, project responsibilities need to be broken into a manageable task of less than a week. Especially in large projects, team members could be assigned functionality that might take three to six months to develop. With pair rotation, this three to six months' worth of functionality would need to be broken into smaller half-day to one-week chunks. Then the owner can recruit partners for these smaller chunks.

Before describing some ways to assign partners, we address a common area of resistance to dynamic pairing. Christopher says, "When I said it would take me three months to develop the GUI, I didn't know I was going to have to spend some of my time helping Kimberly and Brian do their code. I don't have enough time to help them and still get my own work done!" The only way to get over this resistance is to give it a try.

Others might also wish to develop strong bonds with just one or a few members of the team and not to rotate around the whole team. As long as the "rotating team" is not larger than ten, trust and strong bonds can develop because you will be pairing with each other quite often.

Following are the two ways that we've observed successful pair assignments:

- **Short, daily meetings.** Short, daily meetings are a practice of XP and SCRUM, where the entire team stands up for a short, 10–15-minute meeting (this keeps the meeting short, because no one can sit down until the meeting is over). The focus of attention goes around the room as everyone on the team briefly describes what was accomplished the previous day, what problems were encountered, and what needs to be worked on this particular day. Depending on what problems the person is facing or what the person hopes to accomplish that day, the appropriate team member in the room might say, "I'll pair with you on that today," or "I had that problem once too. This morning, I can show you what I did to solve it." After everyone in the room has spoken, hopefully everyone knows what he or she is doing that day and with whom he or she will partner. If not, the manager or team leader can assign the most appropriate pairings from those who are left. (If you recall, our initial scenario in Chapter 1 was an example of one of these meetings.)

  Pair programming aside, these short, daily meetings are very beneficial for team communication. Within this short, 15-minute period, the team is synchronized and ready to go. These daily meetings are a published organizational pattern. This pattern states "A short, daily meeting is an efficient way of transmitting information to the entire team with the minimum communication overhead. This helps overcome some of the tunnel vision problems" (Coplien 2002).

- **Just say yes.** Another method of assigning pairs is that a task owner asks the appropriate team member to pair with him or her for a task. The team member is not allowed to say no. The only question, then, is when they will pair, a scheduling issue. Whoever asks first, goes first. However, if you give help, it is fair to expect help in return (Newkirk and Martin 2002).

Pair Rotation and Knowledge Management

> Our knowledge has legs—it walks home everyday.
> Leif Edvinsson[1]

Good knowledge management techniques are important for employers and employees alike. Truly, it is not advantageous to have all knowledge in any area of a system known to only one person. For the employer, this is very risky because the loss of one or a few individuals can be debilitating. And employees like to take some time off without being bothered with technical questions or problems. By rotating pairs, knowledge is disseminated; employers reduce risk, and employees can relax when out of the office.

Much of the recent investment in knowledge management has focused on using the Internet and creating databases to allow professionals to share documents or compare data. Invaluable knowledge can also be distributed throughout an organization simply by humans sharing insights and ideas with other humans. Pair programming is a mechanism for encouraging this valuable exchange. Through the use of pair programming, organizations can create Communities of Practice (CoP), a group of professionals that develop bonds between each other because they have jointly solved problems together (McDermott 2000). Members of a CoP develop a common sense of purpose and a desire to share work-related knowledge and experience. CoP members gain from each other knowledge that extends far beyond "book learning."

As programmers rotate among the group, they get the chance to get to know many on their team more personally. This familiarity serves to break down many communication barriers. Team members find each other much more approachable. They will struggle with questions or lack of information for less time before getting themselves out of their chairs and going to ask the right person a question because they know that person quite well. CoP enables person-to-person sharing of tacit knowledge, ideas, and insights that are not documented and are hard to articulate; sharing of tacit knowledge takes place daily in the normal course of the programmers' day.

James Euchner, vice president of Nynex's research and development department, reports that CoPs allowed them to reduce the number of days from 17 to 3 days to set up data services for customers (Stewart 1996). This

---

[1] Quoted in Basili et al., 2001.

type of efficiency gain explains why a pair of programmers can complete a programming task in approximately half the time as one solo programmer.

Alistair Cockburn shares the following story from his interview files (Cockburn and Williams 2001):

> When I arrived, I saw a disheartening sight: Bill didn't have a team; he had a random collection of six, bright, talented individuals who didn't work together. They didn't sit near each other; they didn't even like each other. Here is a scene from a weekly staff meeting:
>
> 'Let's talk about pair programming. (Benefits of pair programming enumerated.) <pause> Therefore pair programming is mandatory. All production code must be written with a partner present.'
>
> <An awkward silence descends. Furtive eye glances are exchanged.>
>
> …
>
> Some of the first paired sessions went smoothly. Other sessions were awkward. Communication was serial and parsimonious. I handheld these guys by becoming a third wheel. I encouraged the developers to think out loud (what Ward Cunningham calls *reflective articulation*). This did the trick. They actually began to work together, not just take turns coding.
>
> After about a week, I noticed a remarkable phenomenon. The developers were talking to each other—as people. You really would have to have been there at the beginning to appreciate this. Anyway, I noticed them having real conversations and laughing. They actually began to enjoy and trust each other.
>
> Within several weeks, they became a real team.

It is through "becoming a real team" that pair programming encourages the creation of CoP.

The knowledge management capabilities of pair programming can be summarized by the reflection of Kurt, a manager at a large corporation in North Carolina, via personal communication with Laurie. Kurt hired RoleModel Software to develop software for a strategic business application. RoleModel assigned Duff and Michael to be the primary developers. These programmers followed all the XP practices, including pair programming. After observing them and seeing their remarkable results, Kurt likened pair programming and pair rotation to bees pollinating an orchard. "The pollination of flowers is a 'lucky accident' that happens when bees and other animals accidentally brush against the stomas leaving pollen grains behind."[2] With pair programming, the nuggets of knowledge left behind with pairing partners are indeed "lucky accidents" of the technique. In addition, both partners can then propagate the nugget throughout the team.

When Duff and Michael started working for Kurt, Michael had Web-programming experience, and Duff did not. Duff had much more experience than Michael in building business applications. As a pair, they very quickly developed a Web application with virtually no ramp-up time. Duff learned Web programming through Michael and was productive without much delay. Michael leaned on Duff to identify and deliver the most critical business value. Kurt also reports that from time to time either Duff or Michael was not available. RoleModel substituted another programmer, who was part of its community, in their place. The surrogate programmer paired and again was essentially productive immediately. Pair rotation creates a shared mindset and a symbiotic culture that simply cannot be duplicated when each person works alone on his or her own task.

Pair Rotation and Training

> Not only do you have experience walking out the door,
> you have inexperience walking in the door.
> —Scott Eliot[3]

Adding staff to a project consumes valuable resources of existing team members. Traditionally, new folks are indoctrinated into a team by spending time with a senior person on the team. Perhaps the person spends a few days giving them an introduction to the system, showing them where various things—everything from the cafeteria to the manuals—are. Then, they are often left on their own to perform some task, albeit not an overly complex one, to get started. During this time, they try their best to figure out what's going

---

[2] From http://www.thebeeworks.com/pollinators/index.html
[3] Quoted in Basili et al. 2001.

on and how things work. Ultimately if they can't figure something out, no matter how hard they try, they will get up and interrupt someone to ask for help. Eventually, team members come to be far less reliant on others. However, this interruption-based approach can be a "sink or swim" form of training for the newbie and burdensome to those who are interrupted.

Alternatively, we have found pairing to be a very effective and efficient training technique. When a new person starts with the team, he or she pairs with an existing team member. When the person first arrives, it is best if the partner is a patient, mentoring senior team member, such as the team coach or leader. The mentor must be willing to communicate and to give up some of his or her own productivity to bring the new person on board. Within a few days to a week, the new person can start to rotate around the team to learn the various aspects of the system and to get to know the team members themselves. This also distributes the burden of training throughout the team. However, the people who work with the newbie must realize that they will have some form of reduction in their own productivity. Each person must spend time to slow down and explain what he or she is doing and how the system works, or the training-via-pairing session will be useless and will be very, very frustrating for the new person.

Laurie's graduate student, Anuja Shukla, did some research about the effect of pair programming on training time (2002). She surveyed software professionals on the differences in training software developers with and without pair programming. She received responses from 30 software professionals. Utilizing a model developed by Richard Stutzke (1994), the survey centered around the differences in assimilation time, (the time spent until they become "independently" productive to own their own task without relying heavily on other team members), and mentoring time, (the percentage of the mentor's day that is dedicated to teaching the newbie). Using Stutzke's model, the effort expended on training is giving by the following formula:

$$\text{Training Effort} = \text{Assimilation Time} \cdot (1 + \text{Mentoring Time})$$

Based on the survey, she found the results shown in the following table, which indicate that training effort can be reduced by a factor of two through the use of pair programming and pair rotation.

	With Pair Programming	Without Pair Programming
Assimilation Time (work days)	18	40
Mentoring Time (%)	26	36
Training Effort (work days)	15	37

Alternatively, Alistair Cockburn (1998) recommends a day-care arrangement for training where the development team is split into a "progress team" and a "training team." The progress team is responsible for 85 to 95 percent of the system, and the training team is expected to deliver only 5 to 15 percent of the system. People are transferred from the training team to the progress team as they are ready. Experts are selected from the progress team to aid in mentoring the training team. These experts must have the personality, inclination, and background to train novices successfully. Using this model, the mentoring experts can take turns rotating around the training team, pairing with each in turn. Additionally, members of the training team who are not completely new can pair with each other with better results than if each struggled alone.

Reprisal: Pair Rotation

If each person in the team paired with only one other person on the team, many benefits—quality gains, communication gains, teamwork gains, trust building, and so on—would be realized. However, even more can be gained by dynamically assigning the partners based on the task at hand. Two of these additional gains relate to knowledge management and to training. Pairing is an excellent knowledge management strategy because it breaks down communication barriers between teammates. They get to know each other and each seems more approachable when a question arises. Also, by pairing with many different people, developers learn more about many aspects of the system and more about the programming and tool techniques of many different people. Pair rotation reduces the training time to assimilate a new team member and distributes the burden of training throughout the team.

We highly recommend you work out the logistics of pair rotation to enjoy these added benefits.

References

Basili, V., Costa, P., Lindvall, M., Mendonca, M., Seaman, C., Tesoriero, R., and Zelkowitz, M. (2001). *An Experience Management System for a Software Engineering Research Organization*, NASA Software Engineering Workshop, Greenbelt, MD.

Beck, K. (2000). *Extreme Programming Explained: Embrace Change*, Addison-Wesley.

Cockburn, A. (1998). *Surviving Object-Oriented Projects: A Manager's Guide*, Addison-Wesley.

Cockburn, A. and Williams, L. (2001). "The Costs and Benefits of Pair Programming," in *Extreme Programming Examined*, G. Succi and M. Marchesi, eds., Addison Wesley, pp. 223–248.

Coplien, J. O. (2002). "Daily Meeting," http://i44pc48.info.uni-karlsruhe.de/cgi-bin/OrgPatterns?DailyMeeting.

McDermott, R. (2000). "Knowing in Community: 10 Critical Success Factors in Building Communities of Practice," http://www.co-i-l.com/coil/knowledge-garden/cop/knowing.shtml.

Newkirk, J. W. and Martin, R. C. (2001). *Extreme Programming in Practice*, Addison-Wesley

Shukla, A. (2002). "Pair Programming and the Factors Affecting Brooks's Law," Master's Thesis, North Carolina State University.

Stewart, T. (1996). "The Invisible Keys to Success," in *Fortune*, vol. 8/6.

Stutzke, R. (1994). *A Mathematical Expression of Brooks's Law*, Ninth International Forum on COCOMO and Cost Modeling, Los Angeles.

Other Issues to Consider

Incorporating pair programming into an organization does have a ripple effect on many aspects of a development team. Outlined in this chapter are some additional factors to consider in a move toward pairing.

Performance Appraisals

Traditionally programmers have been measured based on output: "You completed the keyboard, mouse, and video drivers for Window XP on schedule. You had a below average number of defects reported during system test." For obvious reasons, probably because people help each other and it can be hard to isolate who is responsible for which success (or failure), pairing destroys this method of evaluation. Positively, pairing motivates team success over individual success.

But ultimately, almost all organizations rate each individual on his or her performance. We suggest that peer evaluation be factored into individual appraisals. IBM and other companies have been using peer evaluation for years, even without pair programming. So it appears that peer evaluation is useful in its own right. After all, who knows better what employees are really doing than that person's peers? A short form is developed to collect information on the contributions and abilities of a developer. At appraisal time, a specified number of peers are asked to complete the form for the person under review. The manager factors this peer input into the performance appraisal.

Quite possibly, personality conflicts may be present within a team. This can be handled in one of three ways. First, the employee under review could be asked to provide the names of a certain number of peers to evaluate him or her. The manager should know if these are names of work collaborators and not just friends. These people are then contacted for peer evaluations. Second, the manager should use his or her judgment if one peer evaluation provides input that varies widely from the others', input—either positively or negatively. The manager should have the authority to discount a peer evaluation from the final appraisal. A third possibility is to ask the employee under review for a list of names of peers who should *not* be asked for an evaluation. The manager is then free to ask anyone else. Assuming that this list is short, it can be an effective way of making sure that those with personality conflicts do not unfairly slant the evaluation. If the list is long, then something else may be wrong.

An astute manager won't have to wait until peer evaluation time to discover a teammate with a problem. For example, at the end of the daily stand-up meeting, that person might not have been recruited to be anyone's partner; no one ever asks to pair with this person. This can be a signal of any number of problems: personality, hygiene, communication, and so on. Whatever the issue is, it should be pursued to resolution by the manager. This is a good thing, considering the alternative of this lone programmer working (or not) in his or her own cube for days, weeks, or months at a time with some lingering problem.

Group Size

We've been asked many times about the size of a pair programming group. How does pairing scale? How small can your team be? How large can your team be?

To begin, let's consider that with solo programming, the "atomic" unit of a team is one person. How does programming scale with solo programmers? Small, colocated groups need less formal communication. At the other end of the spectrum, large, distributed teams probably need more formal communication. We believe that with pair programming the "atomic" unit of a team becomes two. Other than that, the same scaling rules apply: Small colocated teams of pairs need less formal communication (much of which is done side by side), and large, distributed teams of pairs require more formal communication. Pair programming scales in a way similar to the way solo programming scales.

However, pair rotation puts some constraints on the size of the "rotation group." It's meaningless to pair with a different person daily in your 200-person development team. You never really get to know anyone or anything about the person's code. An ideal rotation group appears be about 10–12 people. With this size group, people can develop personal relationships with their teammates and can get to know all of the code within the group. Often large development teams are broken into group's of this size anyway.

What about small groups? What about groups with odd numbers of programmers? Obviously, the smallest group's size is two. One day, Laurie was at a company that had three programmers on a team doing pair programming. Only two paired at a time, which inevitably left one person working alone. Luckily, the programmers worked in a wonderfully open area. As Laurie talked to the manager, she observed the behavior of the three working in the background. Probably once every ten minutes, the "third wheel" rolled his chair closer to consult with the working pair. The working pair never acted like his interruptions bothered them in the least. They brokered into triplet brainstorming for a short period of time, he rolled away back to his own computer, and they went back to work. It was a beautiful display of teamwork. If you have an odd number of programmers, we'd encourage you to make sure the person who works alone changes daily or sooner. Hopefully, your team will welcome spontaneous collaboration by the person left out, as this team did.

Quality Assurance

Watts Humphrey (1995), describes quality assurance activities, such as code review, design review, compile, and test as filters for defect removal. Depending on the effectiveness of the activity, each filter can remove a percentage of the defects that have been injected, but no filter is perfectly effective (and can remove all defects). For example, if there are 100 defects in some production code, a 50 percent effective code review will find 50 of the defects. Now the code might go on to test with 50 defects remaining. Often testing is not as effective a filter, so perhaps 30 percent of the defects might be found in test, allowing 35 defects to ship to the customer.

Pair programming provides another filter. The more filters the better, if we want high-quality code. It goes a bit beyond that, however. Through brainstorming, pairing can prevent defects in the first place, and, generally, defect prevention is more efficient than the most efficient defect removal filter. Also, pairing can be a very effective defect removal process (filter) as the navigator actively works to identify defects that are injected.

But what about organizations that have formal QA activities and checkpoints? Where does pair programming fit into these checkpoints? First, we've heard of several organizations that do not produce life/safety critical systems that have substituted pair reviews for code reviews; pair programming is a continual code review itself. However, as we discuss in Chapter 26, a piece of research that still must be done is a formal experiment to assess the effectiveness of code reviewing pair programmed code. It is likely that pair programmed code does not need to be reviewed. However, we are not qualified to declare that just yet.

Many organizations have external testing groups (that is, people within the organization, but not the original code developers) that perform test cases based on the original customer requirements and/or the specification. Obviously, when test cases run smoothly, testing goes faster. When testers run into problems each time they turn a corner, testing goes much slower because of the need to document and recreate problems and to discuss them with code developers. We would fully expect that a testing organization that got pair programmed code for the first time would be pleasantly surprised at how smoothly testing proceeded because of the higher quality.

At the start of the project, these external testing groups give an estimate of how much time they will spend executing their test cases. Should these organizations take a leap of faith and decrease their "normal" estimates considering the code will likely be of higher quality? Chapters 4, 5, and 6 talk about the resistance of many people to pair programming; testers will also be skeptical. Seeing is believing. It is likely that the testing groups will want to see the higher-quality code before believing they will actually get it. After all, if they drastically reduce their test estimates assuming higher quality and they don't get it, they'll be working nights and weekends to get their job done.

We would, however, encourage testing groups to estimate a conservative reduction. Remember Parkinson's Law: "Work expands to fill all available time." The testing effort might take the normal amount of time even with higher quality. We'd also encourage you to measure the testing results (something like defects/thousand lines of code) and to compare these to past projects. Over time, you need to gain confidence that testing really will go more smoothly, and numbers will help to convince you of this.

Functional and System Testing

We've also been asked many times whether the testers themselves should pair. We would, in fact, encourage testers to pair as they create their test cases, especially if it involves writing some test code. As we've said before, the more complex a task, the more beneficial it is to pair. Writing test cases can be quite complex. Testers look at the customer requirements and/or specification and need to come up with an execution sequence that attempts to demonstrate whether the requirement or specification has been properly implemented. Then they need to think diabolically about all the possible things users can do wrong as they try to use that functionality so they can make sure the code handles these situations gracefully. Just think how creative a pair of testers can become when they put their heads together and think diabolically! We've also seen that after testers write the test cases together, they tend to execute the test cases separately (although often physically close to each other). When they find a problem, they find a partner with whom to discuss the symptoms and results. Often they first have to determine if the problem is with the test code or with the code under test. Working with their testing partner makes good sense, until the defect is attributed to the code under test. Then the tester should pair with the code developer.

With Extreme Programming, the customers work with the development team to create acceptance test cases. Through a pairing of a customer and a developer, excellent test cases can be created. However, as important, the developer can gain new understanding of what the customer actually wants. Customers often know what they want (the success paths through the code), but they are not as clear about what they might do to make things go wrong (the failure paths through the code). We'd encourage a pair of developers/testers to augment the customer acceptance test cases with failure test cases. (It's a fact of life that these failure test cases ultimately happen in the customer location, so we might as well be prepared.) Remember, think diabolically!

Maintaining and Enhancing Code

We've also been asked about maintaining and enhancing code—does pairing work here? We've done extensive surveying on this topic. All in all, the feeling is that pairing is often as beneficial for maintaining and enhancing code as for writing new code. (Some say that maintenance can sometimes be simple, rote work and pairing is not justified. In these cases, it is hard to keep the navigator engaged.)

Fixing defects and maintaining code can be quite complex and requires detective-like skills. In this case, it is conducive to collaborative problem solving. Two can figure out what is going on better than one can. When a pair discusses what they see in the code, they gain further understanding of what's going on. They can validate (or invalidate) each other's theories about the code. They are also less likely to introduce new defects in the course of their work.

A pair is more likely to make more aggressive changes because their fear of making a mistake is reduced. You know how it is: "I'm not going to touch that code, you touch it." Having another person with you makes you feel more comfortable in making tough decisions.

Many also highly recommended that the pair consist of an original code writer whenever possible. In this manner, code can rapidly be enhanced. Over time the code maintainer will gain greater insight into the entire system from the original coders.

Bob Hartman, vice president of engineering at eSoft explains the results his company has seen from transitioning his maintenance team to pair programming.

> After starting to use Pair Programming, eSoft has an almost-perfect success rate at fixing defects correctly (that is, problem resolved, no other problems created). In our product, QA time is significant, so decreasing it means not only is the product better, but we have also saved money, and in the end the start to finish time on projects is often approximately the same as it was when we did single person programming. Said another way, the gain in QA made up for the loss in time programming with two people.

References

Humphrey, W. S. (1995). *A Discipline for Software Engineering*, Addison-Wesley.

Tips 'n Tricks

Pairing isn't always easy. We've compiled a list of suggestions for making your pair programming experiences as fruitful as possible.

1. Give the driver at least a few nanoseconds to find and correct his or her own mistakes. In addition, give the driver time to find menu choices before giving suggestions or correcting him or her. It gets annoying when someone continually corrects your mistakes, especially typos, when you are about to hit the backspace button yourself. Don't second-guess every keystroke. Some people seem to be able to examine several lines visually as they are typing and are constantly moving back and fixing things while they are pushing forward. Others miss the mistakes as soon as the cursor leaves the area. Be observant and adapt to your partner.

2. If your partner is getting bored or falling asleep, pass him or her the keyboard. If you're getting tired, pass your partner the keyboard. If both of you are tired, try getting up, walking around, or taking a break to stop the infinite loop.

3. If your partner is getting tired or frustrated, grab the keyboard. That's one of the beauties of pairing. When you're tired, you can be the navigator and be freed of the need to type. But, as a pair, you're still moving full steam ahead.

4. In an aim for peace and harmony, it's good to come to an understanding of how pairing will work before getting started with a new partner. Roy Miller of RoleModel Software offers a suggestion: "One of the best tricks I've ever used when pairing is to start each pairing session with some 'negotiation.' I lay out what I like and don't like when I pair with someone, things I do well and things I don't do well, things I need help on, things that bug me to

death. Then I listen while the other person does the same. This takes less than five minutes, usually, but the results are staggering. Both members of the pair then can use the pairing session as a time to get work done and to help the other person. I think 'pairing as negotiation' is a key concept."

5. Ultimately, there will be conflict—on design, direction, and technique—between the partners. (If there's not conflict, then the pairing is experiencing some other form of dysfunction.) There are several ways to handle this disagreement.

One way is for the navigator to record (on cards) contentious issues that are bothering the driver. Periodically, say every half hour, the pair should review the issues. Some of the issues may have disappeared as time passes, others may still need to be dealt with. Recording the issues on cards allows progress to be made and ensures that concerns will be addressed in a focused debate/negotiation.

Another way of handing disagreement is for the pair to separate for a specified period of time, say ten minutes or so. During this time, each of the pair independently investigates his or her desired solution through solo programming, prototyping, or some dedicated pencil-and-paper design time. At the end of the time, the pair gets back together to discuss their investigation. With more information on each solution, hopefully the pair will be able to agree on an approach.

Wayne Conrad offers a variation of this approach. When he's in a conflict, he says, "Just let me drive for five minutes. If you like what you've seen, you can drive it to completion. If you don't like what you've seen, we'll roll back and go in some other direction." This has worked well in practice. Handing a timer to the partner is an important token. It's saying, "I'm not tricking you into letting me drive my idea to completion; I just want to show it to you. By giving you this timer, I'm promising to quit when it goes 'beep, beep, beep' and then let you decide where to go next." It's telling your partner you are not stealing decision-making power.

Ultimately, there should be a team leader/coach/manager who resolves between partners issues that just cannot be resolved on their own.

There needs to be a balance between holding one's ground and compromise. Be assertive without being aggressive. A partner who always gives in to his or her partner's (perhaps adamant) suggestion, is doing a great disservice to the team. Similarly, a programmer who never gives in or never gives his or her partner's ideas a fair chance may as well not be pairing. Pairs that insist on debating every single issue are impeding progress. Choose your battles wisely; save them for issues that really matter.

6. Use a coding standard. This eliminates partner disagreement due to style.

7. Use test-driven development. Test-driven development is an Extreme Programming practice in which programmers write automated test cases (using a test suite like Junit[1]) before writing code. The idea is to write incrementally and iteratively a few test cases, then write a few lines of code to make the test cases pass. Write a few test cases; write some code. You know the drill: Lather, rinse, repeat.

   Several people have said that they really started to realize the value of pair programming once they coupled it with test-first programming. They cite that by writing the test first, both partners in the pair have a more firm grasp on the problem they are solving. In Chapter 8, we talked about Bill Wood and Bil Kleb at NASA Langley who have two displays—one with the test cases and the other with production code. In this way, one of the partners writies the test code, and the other writes production code. They rotate the roles of driver and navigator very quickly as each of them writes test and production code.

   Because so many people profess the coupling of pair programming and test-driven development, we have an introduction to the technique and an outline of its professed benefits in Appendix D.

8. Practice active listening (Helgesen and Brown 1994) by acknowledging, restating, and summarizing ideas and discussion points. Be empathetic toward your partner.

9. Talk a lot. Talk about what you're doing. It helps your partner understand what you're doing, and you might realize a flaw in your logic as you talk. Explain techniques for using the development environment.

---

[1] See: http://c2.com/cgi/wiki?TestingFramework.

10. If your partner is just not listening to you at all, get up and walk away. This is a strong sign of your displeasure that hopefully will help your partner to see the error of his or her ways.

11. Just ask! If you don't understand what your partner is doing, then stop and ask. If you still don't understand, ask again. Ask yourself, "When I get handed the keyboard am I going to be able to carry on doing this?" If not, ask again. "Trust me, it'll work" is definitely not an acceptable answer from the driver.

   In a mentoring situation, the mentor can ensure and enhance the understanding of the learner by asking him or her lots of questions in a pseudo-Socratic dialog (Brignac 1997, Cyrs 1994); the mentor can ask good questions in order to emphasize what is important and relevant.

   By asking questions, you help the driver divulge his or her thoughts at all points. This keeps the pairing more collaborative instead of one person working and one person watching. As we said earlier, in an effective pairing relationship no more than a minute should go by without some form of communication. To accomplish this, there has to be a lot of talking and a lot of asking—oh, and a lot of listening!

12. Take enough showers; eat lots of breath mints. Enough said.

References

Brignac, C. (1997). Effective Teaching in Agricultural and Life Sciences Web Site, http://www.ais.msstate.edu/TALS/unit1/1moduleD.html.

Cyrs, T.E. (1994). *Essential Skills for College Teaching: An Instructional Systems Approach.* Center for Educational Development, Las Cruces, NM.

Helgesen, M. and Brown, S. (1994). *Active Listening: Building Skills for Understanding*, Press Syndicate of the University of Cambridge, England.

Pair Programming Partner Picking Principles[1]

Often, we hear questions like, "It would never be worth it to pair two of your best people together, would it?" "Is there any kind of pairing that just doesn't seem to work?" "It must be very frustrating for the expert who has to spend a lot of time pairing with the junior people. Is that what you find?" "What's the most effective kind of partner to have, someone of equal skill to yourself?" Our response is basically that there are lots of different kinds of pairs—each has benefits and drawbacks in particular situations. So, it's very good to match the makeup of your pair to the task at hand. Need a seemingly impossible algorithm? Put two experts on it. After their morning session together, they'll spend the afternoon completing the patent application. A relatively routine task? Put two novices on it and they'll 'high five' each other as they leave for lunch. Again, a relatively routine task? Put two experts on it and see their blood pressure rise . . . or one of them fall asleep. You get the picture.

There are also pair programming pairs that flat out won't work. If you recognize these situations, make a decision to move toward one of the ones that do work, or maybe to be a maverick (a term Ken Auer of RoleModel Software uses for a solo programmer). Like we said, pairing's not for everyone.

We've also been questioned over and over again about issues such as gender and cultural differences between the pairs. Our experience has shown that these are non-issues. We do recognize that they could become "issues." But if they do, they tend to be very deep-seated problems that go beyond pairing.

---

[1] Title inspired by Peter Piper.

In Part Three, we will guide you through seeing the benefits and drawbacks of various pairings so that you can apply these to your own particular context. We show you when they work and, if there are problems, offer some suggestions on resolving them. Using this information, you can best match your pair to your task to maximize the efficiency of the pair. Or, to know when to disband a pair.

In each chapter, we complete a template for each of these different kinds of pairings. The meta-level template for each chapter in this section is as follows: title, illustration, scenario, descriptive sections, and lastly personal scenarios.

- The title describes the topic area and also indicates if this is a non-issue or a problem area.

- The illustration attempts to give some context for the scenario. These pictures were drawn by a very talented artist, Jennifer Kohnke.

- The scenario provides a sometimes humorous and sometimes poignant discussion of the particular topic area. Most often it shows how *not* to pair program given the particular situation. Let us say it again; these are *usually* how *not* to handle the pairing—they are a (hopefully humorous) look at an exaggerated pair of this type.

For the beneficial pairs, the descriptive section includes the following topics:

- intent—when you should use this kind of pair and what you should hope to see in this type of pairing;

- characteristics of success—how a successful pairing works; and

- challenges—areas that you should watch out for.

The problem pairings includes topics on:

- root causes—what the problem really is;

- general form—how you recognize the problem; and

- refactored solution—what you should do to solve the problem if you happen to have it.

The nonissue section includes these topics:

- issue—a statement about what is the concern

- what this is about; and—more details about the issue; and

- if there are problems—we offer some possible solutions.

Finally, the Personal Scenarios section includes quotes that we received from many practicing pair programmers, including things to do and things to look out for. Many of the quotes in this section of the book came from an extensive Web-based survey of these professional pair programmers. Many thanks to all of you who participated!

Much of this section involves characteristics of people. You should not think of these characteristics as individual people, but roles that the partners are playing. For example, let's look at the expert, average, and novice characteristics. You may know a ton about the area that you are working on and are therefore an expert. On the other hand, you may know some and be comfortable with the area (average) or you may not know anything about it (novice). What is important is that you may operate as the expert, average, or novice role, all during the *same* pair programming session depending on what specific topic area or context you may have to address. For example, you may be the user interface wizard, but during one part you have to do a sorting algorithm and you are only "average" on the various sort options. Steve Hayes suggested a great way to characterize novice, average, and expert: "I can't do it," "I can do it, but can't explain it," or "I can explain it."

Note—in some of these discussions you see references to Laurie or Bob. Yes, we are talking about us, the authors!!!

Expert-Expert Pairing

Martin *(typing)*: If we utilize a list of components here, we will be easily able to scan them in the execution phase. *(He quickly creates a new class instance and begins storing the components.)*

Professor Bob *(watching)*: Yes, but if you make it doubly linked, we can easily manage the operation of finding the previous element, which we'll need later on.

Martin *(typing)*: Good idea. *(He quickly changes the base class to be one that builds doubly linked lists.)*

Professor Bob *(watching)*: Wait! Your crazy trackball highlighted two lines instead of one, and you deleted an important line.

Martin *(typing)*: Damn, I did it again. My RSI (repetitive strain injury, an injury to the hands and arms resulting from the use of computer keyboards and mice) is acting up again. *(He hits control Z to undo the deletion.)*

Professor Bob *(laughing)*: You were the world's worst typist before the RSI. I can't stand to watch you type! Let me drive.

Martin *(mumbles to himself)*: Maybe we can get this speech input thing to work on code?

Professor Bob *(screaming)*: Arrrrrgggggghhhhhh. Give me the keyboard!!!

Intent

To get even the most complex job done well.

As Ron Jeffries of Object Mentor says, "When the two experts get in sync, you can hear the lightning crackling. Working with a good expert partner is like gaining 40 or more IQ points."

Characteristics of Success

As Aretha Franklin sings in the song "Respect," "R-E-S-P-E-C-T. Find out what it means to me." The bottom line to successful expert-expert pairing is respect. When there is mutual respect between the experts, then the sky is the limit for what can be accomplished. The experts can push each other to exceed their limits far better than either one can do alone. Experts don't have to spend much time explaining things to one another. It is almost as if they are on a different plane of existence; they can often communicate using few words. They can be seen examining the situation, rejecting several competing ideas, and quickly zooming in on the best solution. The expert-expert pair can be running with their speedometer pegged at the maximum speed.

As you might guess, running at this top speed can be exhilarating yet, at the same time, quite intense and exhausting. We have observed in expert-expert pairing is a fair amount of joking around and kidding with each other (again, that old "respect" surfaces here, as experts who are kidding around with each other, clearly respect and feel very comfortable with their partners). Certainly, they are having fun, but we feel that it may also be something deeper. The levity is a means of slowing down, reducing the tension, and making the exhausting parts easier to handle. The levity gives the experts time to breathe before taking the plunge into another intense session.

Another successful expert-expert pairing is when the two experts bring very different skills to the problem. For example, when one expert is working on integrating his or her part of the system with a module that is "owned" by another expert, the benefits can be enormous. Having the two experts work together will ultimately lead to a well-functioning integration, often improving the two modules in the process.

Finally, one of the most important benefits of the expert-expert pairs is that the knowledge and learning gained by each of the experts enhance their expertise. It has been our experience that when interacting with your partner you inevitably learn new things. Sometimes you learn about your partner's area; however, more often than not, the experience teaches you something new about your own area of expertise.

Challenges

A significant challenge of the expert-expert pairing is management believing that it is a good idea in the first place. Even managers enlightened to the benefits of pair programming are wary of pairing up their best resources when there are so many problems to be handled. On the other hand, a "super" expert-expert pair can often tackle a problem that is beyond the capabilities of the mere mortals, and they do it more efficiently. Thus assuming that your shop is fully behind the pair programming concepts, we recommend that managers use their expert-expert pairs as their "ace-in-the-hole" for those particularly nasty and difficult problems.

When an expert-expert pairing actually does take place, the biggest single issue seems to be one of egos. It is quite often the case that experts have big egos to go along with their big talents. They might have a "do it my way or the highway" attitude that might lead to severe problems with an expert-expert pairing, or with any pair, as we'll discuss in Chapter 22. If you're an expert and seem to be having trouble working with another expert, do some soul searching. Are you open to learn from them? Are you too concerned about convincing them that you really are an expert? Relax, check your ego at the door, and enjoy your intellectual journey to greatness together!

Personal Scenarios

Bob recalls his first experience at pair programming back in the early '90s while on sabbatical at Hewlett-Packard Research Labs working with Martin Griss, the renowned "Reuse Rabbi" (Jacobson et al. 1997). This was long before they even knew of XP or pair programming. Their setup was not ideal in terms of how the computer and chairs were laid out. (Martin's office has the computer on an inside corner, so whoever played the role of navigator had to sit slightly behind and look over the driver's shoulder.) Because Martin never learned to touch type, Bob was constantly razzing him about his poor typing. Bob and Martin continue to pair program today. It has become even more difficult recently because Martin has a bad case of RSI and has rigged his work environment with large buttons he can press with his palms, and he can use a huge trackball instead of a mouse. However, even with all these challenges, pair programming is truly an amazing experience. There is total and complete respect between Martin and Bob, there are no egos, and they both know and understand each other so well that it truly is two minds thinking as one. From the early experiences with Visual Basic and building a component-based graphical programming system to measurement systems and, more recently, to personal agents, each and every task has benefited from pair programming (in the broadest sense of the phrase, which includes requirements, design, implementation, and test). Both Martin and Bob bring different expertise to the various problems. They tend to feed off one another with the result being high-quality, functional code that often exceeds their expectations. Having experienced it first hand for over a decade, Bob is still amazed at how effective and enjoyable pair programming is.

Martin Griss provides his own viewpoint of their expert-expert pairing:

> Actually, Bob and I go way back. I remember some late evenings in the late '70s at the University of Utah when we were developing a microcoded LISP system on a Burroughs B1700. We came very close to pair programming. Together we would develop pieces of test code in LISP, and one of us would hand compile and assemble a stream of byte codes while the other would type them in "... 5 0 foo ...." In

those days, I could type amazingly fast with two and four fingers, and I fancied myself a great programmer. These days, I am not anywhere as good a programmer (or typist) as Bob, and so we tend most of the time to have slightly different roles, where Bob is much more effective than I at creating complete working systems, quickly. *[A comment from Bob:* Don't let him kid you, he was and still is a great programmer!] When we are not at the same console, I might sit to the side. I tend to work more on trying alternative mechanisms and fragments, either on paper or my machine, and then we work together to integrate the best fragment into our evolving code body. I really look forward to the times Bob comes out and we work together. Usually I am engaged in lots of other managerial or architecture meetings, but when Bob visits, I clear my calendar and am able to focus on this task of creating our composition and work late into the night. It is exhilarating! The way we work feels a lot like playing jazz in a small combo—at times we play together; at other times one or the other takes the lead or alternates in building on an emerging theme. We have an amazing ability to do joint design, complete each other's sentences and code, and work from a preliminary and incomplete vision. We share a philosophy on how systems should evolve and how solutions drive system construction.

Others in our survey described situations that help to illustrate some of the unique aspects of the expert-expert scenario. The first is consultant Wayne Conrad, who suggests that a "more efficient" communication channel is possible between two experts:

Did you ever read the parts of Asimov's "Foundation" series where he describes how the mathematicians communicate amongst themselves? It's like that. I've had conversations with an expert back-seater that go like this:

Me *(Type, type, type, type, type, pause)*: Observer?

Him *(watching)*: Yeah.

Me: OK.

Me: *(type, type, type, type, type, type):* Template method?

Him: Nah . . . too heavyweight here.

Me: Lambda?

Him: Sure.

Me: *(type, type, type, type, type, type, type)*

Expert-expert pairings seem to be especially accelerated. I don't have to explain or justify "routine" practices and ordinary patterns.

Steve Hayes of Khatovar Technology Pty, Ltd. describes roles that often occur within an expert-expert pairing:

> I would say this situation arises whenever you have two people of comparable experience who trust one another. What I find is that the individuals quickly slip into different roles—I'd characterize these as "strategic" and "tactical." The tactical programmer is at the keyboard, worrying about the mechanics of getting the code into the machine. . . . The strategic programmer is thinking about whether the objects are cohesive and loosely coupled, thinking about whether the names are correct, and thinking more about the problem that is being solved. The pairs switch around frequently. If the experts have different areas of expertise, . . . then they oscillate through a rapid sequence of novice-expert pairings.

Labwerks Interactive's A. K. Molteni describes what happens when two individuals who are experts in different areas pair together:

> We were experts in different areas (GUI and Coding). He would start programming and ask about how the interface was going to function. I would take over and make the interface work with his code. Over time we became [so] fluent in each other's expertise that we were able to communicate with great ease. At first it was frustrating as we didn't have the "lingo," but as time went on we developed our own way. The best part was continually being able to get feedback from the client as we always developed both the front and back end in tandem.

Michael Lindner of Sonus Networks describes one of the most important benefits of an expert-expert pairing—new knowledge and learning that an expert gains from the interactions with the other:

> Instead of fighting "religious wars" we found ourselves sharing the experiences that gave us our "religion," with the result that we resolved differences in style, and each learned techniques based on the other's experience.

References

Jacobson, I., Griss, M., and Jonsson, P. (1997). *Software Reuse: Architecture, Process, and Organization for Business Success*, Addison-Wesley.

Expert-Average Pairing

Skip *(an average programmer, driving)*: Let's see, maybe I should use the sum method on this class and munge the result, or then again, I could add a new method to the class itself.

Donna *(an expert, watching, starting to get frustrated)*

Skip *(driving)*: Hum, then again, I could design and instantiate a whole new class whose goal in life is to perform this computation for me.

Donna *(playing with her hair, now highly frustrated and starting to get angry)*

Skip *(driving)*: On the other hand, I recall that there is a library function that does most of what I need, although that will require that I massage the result a bit.

Donna *(pulling out hunks of her hair, red-faced, steam starting to come from her ears, finally explodes, grabs the keyboard and types)*: `result=input1.sum()+ input1.average()/2;`

Skip *(grabs the keyboard back)*: Oh, yeah, that will work, too.

Intent

To get the average job done well, while raising the skill level of one programmer.

Characteristics of Success

There seem to be two types of average programmers. One type is those who have a lot of experience but are, well, just average. The other type is those who are on their way to becoming an expert but simply lack the experience that is typical of an expert. Our experience tends to show that an expert-just average pairing is not very effective. We'll discuss that pairing more in Challenges later in this chapter. However, expert-rising star pairings do work very well and are an excellent method for helping that average programmer become a true star.

As you will see in the next chapter on expert-novice pairing, effective expert-average pairing also requires that the expert do some mentoring and "teaching." The average programmer has sufficient knowledge about programming that he or she can have a good discourse with the expert; it just may require that the expert explain some things more than if talking with another expert. Typically the expert would not have to explain what a pattern is, but he or she might have to explain why a particular pattern is being used in a situation. This is not heavy-duty teaching, but it does require that the expert slow down during the work and explain more of the reasons "why." It is important to realize that there are two kinds of instruction that can go on here. The first is teaching programming, tools, the environment, and the "how we do things in this company." The second is teaching how to pair. It is difficult to teach both of these at the same time. The best training is first to learn how to pair and then move into the how to program.

Assuming that average programmers know how to pair, they must effectively play their role in this relationship. They should not sit silently and watch the expert go about business. Average programmers must speak up, interact, and ask questions. Naturally, they should not become pests and keep asking the same question over and over (this will definitely hurt a pairing). It has to become clear to the expert that the average programmer is "getting it," otherwise the expert will become frustrated.

Another important aspect of this pairing is that the average programmer often brings his or her own experiences to the pairing, and those fresh ideas often stimulate the expert into new, creative solutions to particular problems. Experts are often experts because of their experience and their ability to see a situation and draw from their vast knowledge base to pull out a trick or technique that will solve the problem at hand. The average partner typically has sufficient skill to understand what is currently being designed or implemented and can often see places where his or her own experience might actually lead to a better solution. As long as the experts are not so stuck in their own ways and are willing to listen to ideas from their partners, this can ultimately lead the pair to producing a better asset.

Questions you might be thinking to ask are "Should the expert become a 'professional driver' and drive all of the time? Or should the average programmer drive all of the time?" We'll discuss that in Personal Scenarios. However, we firmly believe that switching driver and navigator is always beneficial. The expert can show tricks and tools that can help improve the speed of the development process. The average engineer can benefit from the expert watching what he or she is doing and providing immediate feedback as to the best way to do things. Hands-on experience is always beneficial.

Challenges

As we see it, there are three situations where the expert-average pairing is a problem. The first is when the average programmer really is average. Quite often programmers like this are good at doing their jobs, but they are not open to expanding outside of their area of expertise. They take assignments that are similar to what they have done in the past, and they tend to work the same way to solve the same kinds of problems. These programmers can be so rigid that learning or even being exposed to new ideas and concepts is a *bad thing*. Pairing an expert with these types of programmers should probably be avoided. The expert will soon become frustrated and might write off the programmer as unwilling to learn.

The second challenge is when average programmers do not interact enough with the expert; they do not ask sufficient questions. An expert who is driving will often simply keep working and assume that his or her partner is following along. Thus opportunities for improving the average programmer's abilities or for explaining why particular decisions are being made will be lost. The average engineer must ask questions when he or she doesn't understand what is going on.

As mentioned earlier, the last significant challenge occurs when the average programmer doesn't seem to "get it." After having something explained once, the average programmer keeps asking the same question over and over again. This can leave the expert frustrated and can reduce the ability of the pair to complete the task. Often, this is the fault of the expert who may not be very good at explaining things. Or maybe the pair simply does not have enough shared background to be able to communicate effectively. In any case, good, clear communication between the members of a pairing, where the average engineer is able to absorb the information, is imperative to making a successful expert-average pairing. We must therefore restate this important point: Communication is a key ingredient in all successful pairings.

Personal Scenarios

Wayne Conrad, a consultant, describes the teaching aspects of the expert-average pairing:

> These can be a lot of fun. There's a lot more teaching that takes place than in expert-expert pairing, so less code gets produced. However, teaching is very rewarding in itself. Sometimes it's hard to have the courage to do this if your boss is measuring only the code you deliver.

The ability of the average programmer to pick up new methods and techniques is exemplified by Michael Lindner of Sonus Networks:

Without really trying, the "average" person picked up a very deep understanding of the system being developed, as well as a toolbox full of useful tools and techniques.

Greg Houston of Internet Security Systems highlights the idea that the average programmer can provide new ideas to the expert:

The average programmer certainly helped a lot. He would call for better explanations that forced me to think through solutions better. In addition, even working with an average programmer, I find they have experience and ideas that add to my own. The "collective mind" of pairing helps create better code.

Finally, Jim Murphy of Ironring Software discusses the importance of the average programmer asking questions:

The average guy could get intimidated easily and not volunteer enough, even when he had good input. It can degenerate into an expert-beginner [pairing] fast if the expert doesn't realize that dynamic. Then the average guy feels marginalized and doesn't have a good experience.

Expert-Novice Pairing

Zeus (*typing very fast*): `x = frobnatz.bar(1, y,`

ScaredLamb (*watching*): Excuse me.

Zeus (*still typing*): What!! `errorNum+`

ScaredLamb (*cowering and watching*): Why did you type a space after the comma?

Zeus (*typing even faster*): That is how I always do it. (*continues typing*) `7);`

ScaredLamb (*watching*): Why?

Zeus (*typing and screaming*): Because, that is how I always do it! Now you drive.

ScaredLamb *(starts to type very slowly)*: `z = frobnatz.mumble(3,4`

Zeus *(screams)*: Noooooo! *(and whacks ScaredLamb in the back of the head)*

ScaredLamb *(whimpering and typing even more slowly)*: `<backspace> <space> 4);`

Intent

To get the easier job done well, while training a novice programmer.

Characteristics of Success

You might be thinking: "Does it ever make sense to pair an expert with a novice?" After all, the expert should be able to solve the problem very quickly, and all you would be doing is slowing the expert down. Well, it turns out that expert-novice pairs can have several advantages. One significant advantage is the training that the novice will receive via apprenticeship. The novice will learn by doing and by watching what the expert is doing. The novice can see the decisions that are being made and ask questions as to why this and that are being done. The novice will gain knowledge about processes used by the team, techniques that can be used to solve various problems in different situations, and how the team does work. This master/apprentice relationship is extremely powerful and one of the best ways for a novice to learn to become a valuable member of the team. Interestingly enough, we've heard the following comment—almost verbatim—from several different development managers: "We used to consider a new person unproductive for their first three months. Now, we find that new people can help out almost immediately."

The apprenticeship can even be valuable for novices who are novices only in the sense that they haven't been with their team for very long. As they might say on Star Trek: "It helps them to be assimilated into the collective (team)." Watching and then doing with an expert by your side can greatly reduce the time it would require to learn "the right way" of working with the team. It really helps when the newbie works with many of the experts (or with any team member) so he or she can learn about many different aspects of the system.

One of the most unexpected aspects of an expert-novice pairing is that the novice actually helps the expert to do a better job. We have had so many people tell us this, that it clearly happens and happens often. Teachers have a saying, "You don't really know it until you have to teach it." Experts can come to a far greater understanding of a technique by slowly and deliberately explaining it to a novice. It usually begins when the expert starts to explain to the novice a decision or a design or even how some code is being implemented. The novice usually asks several questions and often asks the most important question: "Why?" When the expert is explaining what is going on, sometimes the expert realizes that he or she has made a mistake. We believe that this is because the expert slows down and, in the process of explaining something, uncovers an invalid assumption. When the expert is talking, his or her mind is often reevaluating what was done and sometimes a flaw is discovered. We believe that this phenomenon is very similar to the "Tell It To the Furby" method of debugging[1] (see pair debugging in Chapter 3). Sometimes, the listener's understanding does not seem to be relevant. Both methods involve explaining what you are doing, and by simply doing that exercise, better designs or implementations occur and problems are often uncovered. In any case, by slowing down at just the right places, the novice actually helps the expert to do a better job.

Challenges

Clearly, pairing an expert with a novice requires that the expert be able to interact with the novice as a teacher would interact with his or her students. Some of the characteristics of an effective teacher are patience, a willingness to explain, patience, the ability to articulate clearly the work that is being done, compassion for the student, and, most important, patience. (Yes, we meant to put "patience" in there three times.) The expert must also create a comfortable environment that is nonthreatening. This will be highly conducive to making the expert-novice relationship work. So the main problem with this pairing is when the expert is unwilling or unable to teach or interact in a master/apprentice relationship. In addition, if the environment is not comfortable, then the novice will be too intimidated to let the pairing succeed or even to learn at all.

---

[1] This idea comes from Jeff Grigg on http://c2.com/cgi/wiki?DebugByDescribing.

Another problem is when the teacher is not open to listening to advice from his or her apprentice. Assuming the apprentice has any qualifications at all (for example, a college graduate with a degree in computer science), the apprentice can pick up on problems and know the right questions to ask. The expert has to take off his or her "I am all-knowing" mask and work in partnership with the novice.

Personal Scenarios

Our first real-life example comes from Internet Security Systems' Greg Houston. Greg points out that being a novice does not necessarily mean a beginner; the person might simply be inexperienced in a particular technology:

> On my team, this happened mostly where the novice was inexperienced with the technology. However, the novice was not a novice programmer. So, the novice would pick up the skills in the technology very quickly from the expert. Also, the novice would bring in ideas from outside the "box" which sometimes leads to finding better solutions.

Stu Charlton of Infusion Development brings up the "p" word as being of high importance (that is, "patience," for those of you who missed it earlier):

> Lately my job is in mentoring, so I've been doing this a lot. It's pleasant if you view your job as a mentor or coach. If you're trying to beat a deadline, you're not going to like this arrangement. It requires a lot of patience, a great ability to communicate complex concepts, and a dose of humility. But, assuming the novice partner learned something, the rewards are definitely worth the effort.

Consultant Wayne Conrad echoes the importance of the "p" word but cautions that it can sometimes be very difficult to make progress. This is especially difficult when up against the pressure of some deadline.

> These drive me crazy. I have problems becoming impatient with students who don't know enough for me even to communicate with them. With an expert, I can say "Observer?" and get an answer. With an average partner, I can draw some UML and in a few minutes get an answer. With a novice, I first have to explain UML, then explain Observer, and then explain why decoupling the sender from the receiver is good. Only a few times have I been that patient.

The comments by Ironring Software's Jim Murphy are about the importance of the novice learning the subtleties of a particular task; they also mention a psychological trick that sometimes can help the situation:

> This is the best way to get someone into the game. Oftentimes it's the subtle things that experts do that are never discussed. To get things done well and fast, we invoke some features or Web sites or "process patterns" without thinking about them. I have had good luck with excessive positive reinforcment of a novice's work. The reciprocal gains produced by the novice feeling as if he or she is no longer a novice but a real contributor to the team is a good first step in that actually happening.

Ron Jeffries of ObjectMentor mentions that the expert has to involve the novice actively:

> Novices are often afraid to get involved. You need to let them drive or ask them questions that will draw them out. "Do you understand" doesn't work; they'll just say yes. There can be a feeling of slowness when pairing with a novice, but I believe that even the newest novice, in fact, helps me when I pair with him or her. I'd not hesitate to do it.

We conclude with some remarks from Erik Bennerhult of the development firm Lejbrink Bennerhult who describes how both the novice and the expert benefit from the expert-novice pairing. We feel that the following quote really hits home the point that the involvement of the novice actually helps the expert in immeasurable ways:

> Of particular interest here is that not only the novice programmer benefits from this experience, but that the expert often learns just as much from having to explain underlying concepts. This generally leads to interesting discussions, and the novice often has new and unconventional ideas. We must never fear change! The wisdom of experience and the curiosity and openness of the newcomer sometimes lead to creative solutions that break new ground. More than a few of our time's most celebrated artists generated their greatest pieces of work inspired by children who generally knew nothing of what was expected from them and therefore were able to think about concepts in ways forgotten or overlooked by the experienced artist.

Novice-Novice Pairing

First Newbie *(driving)*: `int x;`

Second Newbie *(watching)*: Wait, why are you using *x* for the variable name?

First Newbie: Well, it's the name that I just thought of.

Second Newbie: But why not use *y*? *X*'s remind me of that XOXO thing: kiss, hug, kiss, hug. Yuck.

First Newbie: Hum, I never thought of that, ok let's use *y*'s. *(typing, replacing the variable with y)*

Second Newbie *(watching again)*: Wait, if we use *y*, someone might think of the word "why."

First Newbie *(thinking hard)*: Yes, you're right. Let's use *z*. That isn't confusing. *(typing z)*

Second Newbie *(watching and starts to laugh)*: Hey, I just remembered something.

First Newbie *(stops typing)*: What?

Second Newbie *(chuckling)*: In my software practice class, our professor told us to choose variable names that meant something. I completely forgot about that. You know, that was a pretty good class.

First Newbie *(remembering fondly)*: Yes, I took it the year before you did, and we discussed the same thing. I completely forgot that too. Maybe we should choose a better name.

Second Newbie *(thinking hard again)*: Yes, but what makes sense here?

Intent

To produce production code in a relatively noncomplex area of the project, giving valuable experience to both programmers in the process.

Characteristics of Success

The novice-novice pairing can be effective for helping the programmers learn. Laurie taught a class where the students were learning about several different topics relating to Web-based programming. The class was completely paired. She observed that the students learned the material better and more quickly than she anticipated. In the computer lab, if one partner didn't know something, then most of the time the other partner had the answer. Alternatively, the navigator would be working in parallel, flipping through resource books or class notes to fill in areas they both did not know. Generally, students learning programming languages are very dependent on their professor for technical questions, advice, and debugging. On one hand, answering student questions is a big ego boost as you walk around the room and play hero. However, it can be quite exhausting. With the pairs, though, they were able to teach each other almost everything, and they hardly ever asked for help. Aside from experiencing some "empty nest syndrome," this change was a big relief to Laurie.

How do these observations relate to a business environment? Assuming that the novices have some qualifications—like a degree or experience in programming—they can help each other out. If they have each previously paired with other team members and have knowledge of some areas of the project, they can educate each other. Often, solo newbies work too long struggling to understand some aspect of the project. Often after working too long (because they don't want to bother anyone with a question), they will ask a more experienced team member for help. This struggling time is unproductive time. (During this time, there's also generally a lot of negative self-talk, such as "If I weren't so stupid, I would know this already.") With a novice pair, if they both don't know something, they have the conviction to ask for help much more quickly, get the answer, and move forward.

We must say that there is a strong caveat to this pair learning. There must be a coach, instructor, or mentor available to answer questions and also to help guide the pair. This is described in more detail in the next sections. We feel very strongly about the need for a coach. If you are unwilling to assign the mentoring task to some expert, then you need to understand the limitations of the asset being produced by the pair. Without this, you can't count on the quality of the work that the pair produces, although it will certainly be higher than that of either of the novices working alone. The novice pair will certainly gain valuable experience and will learn a ton!

Challenges

Since novice programmers by definition lack experience, it is quite easy for them to go down a wrong path, focus on something that is not important, or spend time spinning their wheels on trivialities. Sure, they will still experience pair pressure and not spend time surfing the Web, answering e-mail, and so on; but their progress on the task at hand can be limited simply because neither of the pair has the experience necessary to do an effective job. This challenge can be so great that many people we have surveyed say that they simply do not let two novices pair together. This said, we still feel that a novice pair is a better alternative to a solo novice.

Personal Scenarios

Our first example shows that pairing novices can be effective and particularly rewarding. Dr. Mike Lance of Christchurch Polytechnic Institute of Technology describes how novice pairs know when to ask for help instead of wallowing around trying to find a solution:

> Students work very happily when they are at the same level. They both make the same mistakes and learn to pick them up together. A joint decision to ask for help is often made quickly and decisively. "We don't know what we are doing, do we? Let's get help." Students working by themselves take longer to figure out that they are doing something nonproductive.

Professional programmer Norman Rekitt supports the idea of a good coach available for questions:

> This is probably the biggest challenge. But with the right attitude it works great. You both become experts quickly if you have a good coach.

Many of the survey participants said that pairing novices was a really bad idea and they didn't do it. The first opinion comes from Ron Jeffries of ObjectMentor who says it just doesn't work:

> I think novice-novice is the most problematical. Blind leading the blind. 10 times 10 is 100. 1 times 1 is just . . . 1. I generally advise teams to avoid the novice-novice combination as much as possible.

Stephanie Ward of Interliant points out that there is some good via pair-learning, but the assets produced are usually not that great:

> I think this was a good experience for the two novices, because they were forced to come up with design ideas and figure out how to implement them. However, I found that I couldn't trust the development that came from that pair. It took much longer for them to finish a task, and they slowed down other pairs (understandably) by asking lots of questions. They also didn't seem to have a good grasp of what they had actually done, so knowledge transfer to experts was difficult.

The last point by Steve Hayes of Khatovar Technology Pty Ltd. is quite interesting. Steve basically says that if you can't do an expert-novice pairing, then at least pairing novices is better than simply leaving them to struggle alone:

> In general this isn't great for the project—it would be much better to split the novices up. However, it's interesting to compare novice-novice pairing to leaving the novices working alone. The pairs will produce better code than the same novices working alone. The novices are likely to have different strengths and weaknesses, so they should reinforce one another. They'll end up with a lot of questions—places where they don't agree, but they can't be sure which one of them is right, so it's important to have someone available to answer questions for them.

Extrovert-Extrovert Pairing

Sir Peter and Sir Joseph are standing in front of their computer, developing code for a new subsystem.

Sir Peter (*speaking in a soprano voice*): If we use'th the dec-or-ra-tor pattern, this code will blast'th off to Saturn.

Sir Joseph (*responding in a slow, deep baritone voice*): Me doooonnnnn'tttt think'th so, that pattttteeeerrrrnnnn's really got to go.

Audience (*gasps*): ooooooouuuuuuhhhhh.

Sir Peter (*still squeeking*): Kind'th sir, thy reasoning is quite faulty. That pattern here doth be quite sultry.

Audience (*murmurs*)

Sir Joseph (*responding, but yelling this time*): Ah, my friend, me must grant. Thou art a mangled hasty-witted miscreant.

Swords are drawn and a fight ensues.

Audience (*standing and clapping*): Bravo! Bravo!

Intent

After long, thoughtful, constructive discussions, an excellent creative solution is created.

Characteristics of Success

As you might imagine, pairing extroverts can be tremendously advantageous. Pairing is all about communication, and extroverts typically are among the best communicators. They can discuss the issues and banter back and forth about ideas. They will often openly question decisions, but ultimately they will jointly arrive at the best solution.

Challenges

Extrovert-extrovert pairing is often loud and full of laughter. This should be encouraged, if one is in a large room where the pairing development is occurring (as often used in XP). However, extrovert pairs might spend too much of their time talking, discussing, and arguing. If they are not productive, then the pairing will fail. Therefore it is important for the manager to observe these extrovert teams and make sure that good, productive work products are being produced. Extrovert pairs need to be self-disciplined enough to limit each discussion to a specific number of minutes. It is true that some people just can't seem to stop talking, so pairing in general will not work for them. (In our experience a lot of these people seem to end up being academics.) ☺

Note: In Laurie's University of Utah experiment, she paired two extroverts (to no surprise, there were very few of them in the class). These two spent considerably more time to complete assignments than any other pair; they were outliers in the distribution of time spent. As a matter of fact, the 15 percent more time spent by pairs would have likely been much smaller if it was not for this one pair. This pair freely admitted that they had trouble stopping conversations about what went on the night before and how hard their operating system exam was, and so on—conversations that were totally irrelevant to completing the assignment. It was one long continuous coffee klutch. Watch for this, and figure out how to shut them up and get them to work.

Personal Scenarios

It is often the case that extroverts enjoy being with other extroverts, as described by Eric Herman:

> This is great. Amazing feedback loops! When you get me together with another "talker," we can really make things happen!

Vera Peeters of tryx discusses how much fun extrovert pairs have—maybe too much:

> Lots of laughing. Lots of noise.

Ron Jeffries of Object Mentor agrees:

> Love it. It's more fun, a barrel of laughs. Confident pairing leads to easier exploration and more creative solutions.

This is supported by Matthew Cooke of Connextra. He does caution that it is important that management understands what is going on and sees what is being produced and does not worry about how it was produced:

> Much more enjoyable, therefore, more productive. Can concern management as developers are clearly not supposed to be laughing and having fun.

Professional programmer Jason Rogers relates a funny story about how both extroverts tend to be aggressive and want to take control of the project, the overall benefit being that a lot of good work gets done:

Person One: I wanna drive.

Person Two: Then get in your car.

Person One: Ha ha. Seriously, I wanna type.

Person Two: OK. Let's see; I'd say you're a type A.

BANG!!!

Person One: I.S. Department? Hi, this is Person One. I need a new keyboard down here.

Seriously, they both tend to want to drive! So, the keyboard switches a lot. That's a good thing around here.

Several people mention the problems that can occur when pairing extroverts. Jeff Langr of Object Mentor discusses the problem of too much arguing and how one should set some kind of time limits:

They get contentious with arguments if they are opposed to a given direction. Cut all discussion off at an arbitrary mark, say five minutes.

Stephanie Ward of Interliant points out the good and bad of extrovert pairs:

This has both good and bad aspects. I've seen this pair have thoughtful technical discussions that led to better solutions. However, this can lead to long discussions that go nowhere.

Jim Murphy of Ironring Software mentions the psychological aspects of having so much fun that sometimes you don't want it to end:

Fun. Very comfortable feeling resulting from sharing even silly details about how we do work. This is a very rewarding feeling. Sometimes a feature can take longer than necessary because I am having so much fun working on it that I don't want to move on and stop working with my extroverted pair!

Dave Chaplin of Byte-Vision Ltd. also describes some of the problems of pairing extroverts and also offers some interesting solutions on how to solve them:

They can spend a little too much time chatting about what they did over the weekend, rather than getting the job done. Getting them to buy into the timescales normally does the trick. They also tend to be more focused on the happy flows of code and don't like to test as much—being a little too optimistic in the solution they produce. Making a set of unit tests part of the deliverable and reviewing those tests before they code solves this one.

Extrovert-Introvert Pairing

Extrovert *(talking loudly and gesturing)*: Why, this is the easiest problem that I have ever seen. We just call our little, old library function here . . .

Introvert *(quietly watching, shakes his head no)*

Extrovert *(still talking loudly)*: . . . Then if we run the SQL query right here, . . .

Introvert *(still watching, shakes his head no)*

Extrovert *(continues)*: . . . Now, we call openPodBayDoors to handle . . .

Introvert *(still watching, still shaking his head no)*

Extrovert *(continues, but notices the Introvert)*: What?

Introvert *(he points to the 87th line and speaks very quietly)*: Incorrect.

Extrovert *(nods his head and continues talking)*: That's right, good catch. I need to use the other library function. Now, what we need to do is . . .

Intent

To allow each partner to draw on his or her strengths and to improve upon his or her weaknesses.

Characteristics of Success

Introverts just don't interact as "loudly" as extroverts. To no surprise, a lot of introverts end up being programmers. We suspect that there is something comforting about sitting in a darkened cube at 3:00 in the morning and beating down the last bug in some product.

Let's assume that we have two talented people; they are just different in how they "interact." When this happens, then the pairing can work. But it takes time for the partners to learn to work with each other. Introverts need to learn to speak up when it is important; likewise, extroverts need to learn to shut up. When this happens, it can be a very good pairing. Each gives up a little of what he or she is, but is still able to be what he or she is. The pairing works.

The key to making this partnership work is for each partner to recognize his or her own personality. Extroverts must consciously work not to talk all of the time. They can use their "extrovertedness" to draw valuable information from their partner; they must ask questions of their partner. We have heard of extroverts who are driving to make mistakes intentionally just so their partner will catch them and learn to "open up." Likewise, introverts must push a little and work to interact. When they see a problem, they must speak up. If there are issues that they don't understand or don't agree with, then they must speak up. They have to learn to express themselves and to let their talents show through.

Challenges

As described earlier, the major challenge of this pairing is that each partner must give up a little to learn to pair. The extrovert must back off from talking all of the time and the introvert must learn to speak up about whatever issue is at hand. The pairing will not work if both do not give a little. Either the extrovert will monopolize everything, and there will be no input from the introvert, or the introvert will be silent and will not interact, thus losing all benefits from pairing.

The other challenge is if either partner uses his or her tendencies to cover up deficiencies. If this is happening, then it is very difficult to make the pairing work. The partner must treat it like an expert-novice pairing and will have to take a much more mentoring role in the relationship. Again, if this is not recognized, then the pairing will not succeed.

Introvert-Introvert Pairing

Danny *(typing very fast)*

Laurie *(watching)*

Danny *(still typing very fast)*

Laurie *(nudges Danny and nods)*

Danny *(recognizes and moves the cursor to the third line and makes a change)*

Laurie *(smiles and keeps watching)*

Danny *(moves back to the original location and keeps typing)*

Laurie *(points to the fifth line)*

Danny *(moves the cursor up to the fifth line and makes a change)*

Intent

A silent intensity leads to rock-solid solutions.

Characteristics of Success

Many programmers are introverted to some degree. We don't have hard statistics on it, but the majority of programmers are of Meyers-Briggs personality type INTJ (Keirsey 1998, Keirsey 2002)—where the "I" indicates "Introverted." (In Laurie's classes, she's noticed that between 50 and 75 percent of her students have an "Introvert" Meyers-Briggs personality type.) Since many programmers are introverted to some degree, the introvert-introvert pair will be quite common.

Introverts can be fairly quiet and private. They tend to keep to themselves and enjoy isolation. Keirsey calls introverts "reserved"—quick to listen and slow to speak (extroverts, on the other hand, are characterized as "expressive"—quick to speak and slow to listen). Introverts often have a quiet intensity and excel at the demanding task of programming. The intensity allows them to focus on the task at hand and to work diligently to solve whatever problems they are given. Having two introverts tackling a problem can really be successful if you can overcome their natural tendency not to communicate with their partner. Pair programming works when the pairs are tightly integrated, interacting, and working closely. The natural intensity of introverts makes interaction a low priority. Thus the pair has to work to maintain a decent level of interaction. Having a pair of introverts who know each other well can be a real thing of beauty. Often there is not a lot of verbal communication, but the pair learns how to communicate via other means.

We have found that pairing an introvert with another introvert is an effective means of introducing someone to pair programming. If an introvert's first pairing experiences are with a very extroverted person, he or she might find the situation overwhelming or find it hard to get a word in and decide to give up trying. However, they won't have this "competition" to talk with another introverted person. Instead, intorverts might have a competition on who will be the *first* to talk. Through pairing in this nonthreatening way, the introverted person can learn to jell constructively with another programmer—asserting opinions and questions in a positive way. Once they learn how to do this, introverts might be better prepared to be assertive with a more extroverted partner.

Challenges

The difficulty of this pairing is that introverts can be very poor communicators. As you have seen in much of the text prior to this chapter, pair programming is all about communicating. If there is no communication, there is no pair programming. As some of the stories related in the personal scenarios section will show, this is a very difficult issue to overcome. The best solution seems to be to keep on pairing and to let the introverts get to know each other. Once that happens they open up and become much more productive.

It is also important that the manager who arranges this kind of pair keeps an early eye on the partners. Experience has shown that during this "longer pair-jelling" period, the pair is sometimes not very productive and often ends up going down the wrong paths because they are not interacting and questioning each other. A good technique for the manager or other technical lead is to interact with the pair often, see what they have been doing, and make sure that they are progressing.

Finally, a lot of introverts would rather be locked away in an office by themselves, working intensely on a project, emerging only when it is done. Many times, they will strongly resist pairing. We recommend that the manager takes it slowly, pair a little at a time until the pair becomes comfortable with the concept. It is certainly the case that some introverts will resist so strongly that they will never be able to pair.

Personal Scenarios

As you might guess, we have several stories of successful introvert pairs and stories of unsuccessful introvert pairs that did not work out as well. However, the first from Dr. Mike Lance of Christchurch Polytechnic Institute of Technology makes an excellent point of what we mean by the term "introvert":

> Introverts tend to be intense and have lots going on inside their heads. This would be the typical programming student personality profile. Introvert is not the same as low in social skills. . . . Not a noisy group, but happy to do something task-focused.

Todd Jonker of Inpath Solutions talks about how the bottom line is communication between the pairs:

> Gotta open up! This can work if the coders are comfortable with each other. Might be hard if they're both shy and strangers.

Both Jeff Langr of Object Mentor and Christian Wege of DaimlerChrysler AG mention the problems when an introverted pair does not go seeking help. As we stated earlier, this implies that the technical lead should seek out the pair and make sure that they stay on track:

> Tends to be quiet; not as much communication between the two as should occur. They are less likely to raise their hand to the other developers if they get bogged down. Much like the novice-novice pairing, the introvert-introvert pairing should be avoided. *(Jeff)*

> In a workshop such a pair was going in the wrong direction for a long time. They didn't approach the coach early enough and didn't question the partner's work enough. *(Christian)*

Roy W. Miller of RoleModel Software, Inc. provides an excellent illustration of our point that if you work at it, you can get an introverted pair to work and work well. What is interesting about this scenario is that one of the partners (Roy) recognized the difficulty of this particular kind of pairing and worked hard to make sure that the pair was successful:

> One of the guys at my company is usually very quiet, and people give him quite a hard time about it. The first time I paired with him, he just didn't talk. I'm introverted myself, so I fight it by forcing myself to engage people. I asked questions but got no answers. So, I increased the frequency of my questions. Still nothing. By the end of the session, there was a steady stream of questions pouring from my mouth, and my introvertd partner was noticeably frustrated with me. Over time, he and I

have gotten to know one another outside of work. In developing that relationship, we have talked about the good and the bad of pairing. We have talked about how we pair. Now, he and I pair rather well. It took a longer "negotiation" with him to get to the point where our pairing could be productive, but it was worth the effort.

References

Keirsey, D. (1998), *Please Understand Me II*, Prometheus Nemesis Book Company.
Keirsey, D. (2002), "The Keirsey Temperament Sorter II," http://www.keirsey.com.

Gender Nonissue

Alex *(playing a shoot-em-up video game)*: Die, you alien turkeys!

Chelsea *(arrives)*: So, looks like you have everything ready for our pair programming session.

Alex *(sheepishly puts the joystick away; spends several minutes bringing up the text editor and design document)*: Sorry. I was just getting my fingers warmed up for our session *(chuckling)*.

Chelsea *(concentrating)*: So, when we left off, we were going to add our own state machine processor.

Alex (*pointing*): Yeah, let's use the server department's state machine code and just build one right here.

Chelsea (*nods her head*): Yes, I concur.

Alex (*begins to type*): Initial state is cash; the transition triggers on the first payment . . .

Julie, the manager (*walks in*): So, Chelsea, how's it going?

Chelsea (*gets up to talk with their manager*): It is going great; we have most of the code done. Now we are adding some state machine control.

Alex (*reaches over and grabs his joystick*): Got'em!

(*Chelsea and Julie look down at Alex and both shake their heads.*)

Julie: Alex!

Alex (*looks up*): What? What?

Issue

Gender is not an issue.

What This Is About

You might wonder why we even bother to have a chapter on gender issues (male/male, male/female, or female/female pairs). After all, our profession is relatively young, and it would seem highly enlightened. The gender of each member of the pair should just not matter! Well, we added this chapter because we have been asked about it, and it might be a question that you too have. The bottom line is that it really does not seem to matter. What really matters are the same issues that we have addressed in other chapters in Part Three: the similarities and differences in partners' skill levels; how outgoing the partners are; and whether there are problems related to professional driving (see Chapter 21) or egos (see Chapters 22 and 23). So, a successful pairing is based on these characteristics and not on gender.

As we have stated many times before, communication is a key ingredient to successful pairing. We have observed that men and women communicate differently. Generally speaking, men attempt to convey information; they speak mostly about things. Women communicate to receive information or to improve relationships and speak mostly about people (Glass 1993). It is important to realize that there are real differences in communication methods, to recognize them, and to handle them effectively.

If There Are Problems

About the only problem that we can envision is one related to gender disrespect. Should either gender disrespect the other, problems are likely. Because pairs work so closely together, this type of gender chauvinism could become more noticeable and become a real problem. However, it is likely that gender disrespect issues would surface in any team-based situation and thus does not seem to be specific to pair programming. Should these issues arise, we see no solution but to recommend some type of counseling for those with a chauvinism problem. We feel that this kind of bias has no place in the work place in particular nor in society in general.

Personal Scenarios

Our Web survey asked about issues relating to male/female and female/female pairing. This first set of observations is about pairing between males and females. Most of the answers from both males and females echoed words similar to those of Vera Peeters of tryx:

> Sorry, I do male-female (almost) all the time. I don't see what's special about it.

Stephanie Ward of Interliant mentions that other issues are what is significant (such as personalities) but goes on to mention that in her experience some strong positives come out of the pairing because of different ways of approaching problems. We are not convinced that these differences are really gender related or related to other factors such as educational background. But in any case, her comments are highly relevant:

> This is an interesting balance to have, and it can cause problems depending on the personality types. The males on my team are pretty forceful with ideas and will tend to interrupt, while the females are less willing to interrupt and insist on their

ideas. However, I have found males and females approach problems differently, which has always been a positive for me when working as a pair.

As mentioned by Steve Hayes of Khatovar Technology Pty Ltd., gender issues can appear outside of pair programming:

> My first few months of pair programming were done in a male-female pair (I was the male). I've also worked closely with women in the past. Everything went smoothly, and I didn't notice any issues. Later I worked as a coach with a team of five males, and we added a woman to the team. It was clear that there were issues. What still isn't clear to me is how much of these issues were gender based, and how many of them were just accounted for by the individual personalities without introducing gender. I have a sample of only one to work with! Here's my working model: In general, male programmers don't give as much credence to female programmers as they do to other males. The women feel ignored, and they either back down or become quite aggressive in pushing their views. In my group we tried to get everyone to listen better and be more respectful of opinions. Since this is what we needed to do regardless of whether our problem was gender based, we didn't pursue the gender issues any further.

We conclude the discussion on male/female pairing with the comments from Sonus Networks' Michael Lindner who humorously commented that there are other good things that might come out of pair programming:

> We got married, although I don't think it's a result of pair programming.

Another question that we asked was related to problems or issues with female/female pairing. Unfortunately, we had very few responses—most likely due to the sad state of computer science where so few females decide to take it up as a profession. Nevertheless, the comments of these two individuals support our premise that gender simply is not relevant in determining pair performance.

Ron Jeffries from ObjectMentor mentions that basically it isn't clear that gender has to do with the issues. Usually what is based on the skills and/or personalities of the individuals and not on their gender:

> I've seen them work fine and have seen them fail. I'm not sure gender had anything to do with it.

Interliant's Stephanie Ward concurs that although there were issues, it is most likely that the skills of the individuals drove how the pair performed:

> My only experience with female-female pairing was when at least one of the two was a novice, but I found that there always seemed to be some questioning going on. Comments like "Well, what do you think about this?" or "Is this right?" looking for some sort of confirmation, seemed to be the general atmosphere. I found the pair was about compromise and harmony rather than standing up for a particular idea. But one could attribute this to the fact that the programmer was a novice rather than because the programmers were female.

References

Glass, L. (1993). *He Says, She Says: Closing the Communication Gap Between the Sexes*, Putman Publishing Group.

Culture Nonissue

Cowboy Tom (*at the computer, typing*): Whew, doggy, this is some tricky code.

Joelle (*observing*): Comment?

Cowboy Tom (*still typing* `import com.udn.propmanager.*;`)

Joelle (*looking confused*): Ça veut dire quoi "udn"? Est-ce que nous n'utilisons pas les outils de IBM?

Cowboy Tom (*looking at her*): Huh? What? I don't parlez-vous.

Joelle (*shakes her head and points*): IBM!

Cowboy Tom (*nods his head*): Yeah, IBM is a good company, but so what. What are you upset about?

Joelle (*reaches out and points*): *Vous devez utilizer "ibm" au lieu de "udn" ici.*

Cowboy Tom: What the heck are you talking about, little lady?

Joelle (*starts to shout*): IBM, IBM, IBM!

Cowboy Tom (*starts to ignore her and looks back at the screen*): Hey, lookee here, I typed the wrong thing. Must have had my hands shifted over (*he backs up and replaces the udn with ibm*).

Joelle (*shakes her head*): *Ah, quel idiot.*

Issue

Having pairs with different cultural backgrounds is wonderful for building trust and communication within the team. As long as there is communication, the pair can succeed.

What This Is About

In a manner similar to the concerns of the gender chapter, we are often asked the question, "Does the cultural background of the pairs matter?" For example, can someone from Germany work with someone from California? Can someone from the Orient work with someone from India? The bottom line is that cultural background does not matter as long as the pairs can communicate well—that is, both verbal and nonverbal communication. Since we have hit you over the head with the importance of communication, the fact that the key is communication is probably not surprising to you. All of the other issues discussed previously are what is important: the relative strength of the skills and experience brought to the table by each partner and the partners' extrovert or introvert tendencies. Culture does not seem to have an effect on a successful pairing.

We've mentioned how pair programming and pair rotation enhance teamwork and communication. We've found them to be particularly effective when it comes to learning about each other's culture and eliminating cultural barriers. Humans find comfort in being with others like themselves, hence the adage, "Birds of a feather flock together." Unfortunately, this can lead to nonmalicious, nonintentional segregation. For example, there are many Indian students at North Carolina State University. You will generally find Indian students talking with other Indian students. The Indian students will know more Indian students in majors outside of Computer Science than do Computer Science students from the United States or other countries. Or, consider a programmer from China who joins a team of programmers in the United States. He may feel very alone, struggling with English as a second language. Pairing (and pair rotation) encourages us to build bridges and to draw everyone into "the group." We can break down the nonmalicious, nonintentional segregation that tends to happen. When we sit next to each other for enough hours—we'll find out it's Chinese New Year that day—and that it's really not as hard to understand him talk as we thought it was. Or, someone will bring a special food from their country to share. Not only are cultural differences not an issue, they can be a means for learning and celebration.

If There Are Problems

It certainly is the case that there could be some sort of cultural bigotry that could exist in either partner. It is possible that pairing might make this kind of problem surface more quickly since the problem partner would be forced to interact very closely with his or her partner. Without the communication and respect that pairs should show for one another, the pairing would be doomed. Naturally bigotry should not be tolerated in any form. If pairing raises the issue sooner, then that is probably good. There is no place for bigotry in a collaborative environment, and if pairing helps to make this surface sooner, then so be it. The team will be much better off without the bigot.

One of the important comments that is mentioned in many of the personal scenarios relate to what we'll call "personal style." Issues, such as when one comes to work, how long one can work, how often and when breaks are taken, how long is spent on lunches, and so on, arise. In general, these are not true cultural differences; they are personal style issues. The solution is fairly easy but may be hard to implement. It requires that the programmers learn to be a bit more flexible and adapt to their partners—maybe taking fewer breaks or loosening up and actually taking a longer lunch hour to become more socially engaged with your partner. Discovering that these style issues exist requires that each partner spend a little time in self-evaluation of the pair and observe how well the pair is performing. Pretend that you are disembodied, floating around the cube, and be aware of what is happening. This will allow you to "see" what issues your pairing may be faced with and show you where you need to work to take corrective actions.

Maybe the words of consultant Jim Murphy ring true:

> Canadians are the best programmers in the world (pair or otherwise), probably because we have no culture.

Personal Scenarios

Several of our personal comments suggest that culture really doesn't matter. The first comes from Ironring Software's Jim Murphy:

> My experience is that these factors may affect the rate of adoption or initial productivity, but once the ice is broken, these cultural issues are much less visible. Software is description, and we use metaphor to help us describe and talk about our descriptions. These metaphors are often culturally biased in a way that could make it tougher for a team to jell, at least until the team has created a microculture of its own.

Christian Pekeler of CodeFab, Inc. concurs. He also mentions that culture is certainly an issue when interacting, but there is no place for it in pair programming.

> I'm from Germany, working and pairing here in the United States with my colleagues which includes a developer from Japan. And I have also paired a little with someone from France. I do notice cultural differences every day. But none of these differences was or is specific to pair programming. Pair programming means interacting with a partner and therefore forces both to deal with their differences. It can be interesting, but it doesn't really matter whether these differences are of cultural origin.

Professional programmer Jason Rogers provides supporting evidence for the language issue:

> I noticed a few problems in our team when people with very thick accents were paired with others who were not used to dealing with that on a regular basis. The partner with the thick accent would get frustrated trying to communicate, while the other got frustrated because the former couldn't communicate as well. This got better over time, as we all learned to "interpret" what the other was saying, but you can imagine that in the beginning it took quite a while to break down those communication barriers.

Some comments from Lee Lichtenwalner who has spent a good deal of his career traveling around the world follows. He mentions that we should not be so naïve that we think that there are not cultural differences. He points out a number of observations of cultural phenomena that he believes can have some effect on pair programming. We agree that there are differences, but none so large that it really matters. When the pair is focused on solving a problem and meeting a deadline, that is their focus, and culture just isn't an important issue. Some of his examples include the following:

> The German culture is largely one of independence and high quality. While Germans work well in a team environment, they dislike situations in which they cannot stand out for their contributions to the team. Thus I am not sure they hate to pair, but they may dislike pairing if a certain level of recognition is not given to each individual as well as to the pair.

> Italians are a close-knit group with a level of intensity that makes most Americans uncomfortable. They have a strong tendency to sit close together in such a way that it invades the typical space bubble or comfort zone that Americans are used to.

> Indians (from India) tend to be focused narrowly on accomplishment and may dislike American methods of pair programming. . . . However, the American work ethic has a strong dislike for anything over 8–9 hours per day. By contrast, many Indians may thrive only after working 12–14 hours and feel like they have not contributed to the team by doing anything less.

Kent Beck of Three Rivers Institute has observed that there are cultural issues, but they can be overcome by both partners working at building that pair relationship. The body space issue is how close the pairs sit when interacting. He has observed that some cultures are such that close, physical contact is how person-to-person interaction takes place, while others believe, more distance is important. Again, finding a mutually acceptable compromise is the key:

> Body space is only one of many cultural issues that enrich pairing. If I pair with someone from M.I.T., I expect to argue and fight and claw and push to get action. If I pair with someone from the Midwest, I have to draw out conflict. Some cultures talk about personal stuff before they talk about work. Others just start working.

Several comments addressed the strong benefit from working with others with different backgrounds. Erik Bennerhult of the development firm Lejbrink Bennerhult describes how cultural diversity is a real benefit in the workplace:

> Actually, all this diversity was almost only beneficial. People had different ways of going about solving problems. People discussed in different ways. It was really good. It is my firm belief that diversity is good. I also believe that the current state of this business, with only white males from the same socio-economic group is one of the biggest problems in the industry.

Professional programmer A. K. Molteni offers a highly insightful description of his cross-cultural experiences. What is fascinating is how one grows by way of these experiences:

> The cultural issues I encountered did not deal with the programming skill or the pair programming part. When I was part of it, we were both focused on making the best possible product. The culture issues happened outside of work. My work ethic is to get in earlier than most and start working. Taking breaks is kept to a minimum, but lunch breaks are always taken away from the workplace. Pair programming meant I would sometimes have to wait for my partner to show up in the morning. If my partner came in late, he or she would work through the lunch hour, which I wasn't keen on. My partner took longer breaks and took that time to socialize a lot more with other coworkers who were also taking a break. They would also stay late at night, but that's probably because we were all single. The married people kept to

regular schedules. At first it was annoying but eventually we would come to a fine medium. My other group members would start coming in at a scheduled time so we knew we could expect them. We knew who had to go home when, and I started taking social breaks with them. We didn't let go of our own work ethics but incorporated the ones of others. It has made us that much more flexible. The best part of it all was we would understand and respect the coworkers more when they observed their religion/cultural activities (e.g., Lent, Ramadan, Holy Week).

The Professional Driver Problem

Pro Driver *(typing very fast)*: Ah, Grasshopper, if you can take the keyboard from my hand, then you will be the master.

Grasshopper *(reaches for the keyboard)*

Pro Driver *(deftly moving the keyboard to the left while still typing)*: You must be much quicker than that, Grasshopper.

Grasshopper *(observes the typing and tries a feint to the right and a grab from the left)*

Pro Driver *(grabs the keyboard by the escape key and lifts it up three inches)*

Grasshopper *(gets nothing but air)*: Damn!

Pro Driver *(typing even faster now, using her elbows)*: Grasshopper, that is the oldest trick in the book.

Grasshopper *(excitedly points)*: Hey, look at what Jerry left on his monitor!

Pro Driver *(expertly typing with her feet)*: Grasshopper, no, I was mistaken, *that* is the oldest trick in the book.

Root Causes

The desire for power, a driver's lack of confidence in the navigator, a navigator's lack of confidence in him- or herself.

Note: A professional driver pairing may not be a problem if the driver is compensating for a physical or temporary limitation of his or her partner.

General Form

Our problem child is always at the keyboard. Some individuals and some teams have been hurt by a bad professional driver. Let's chat about this "bad" professional driver. Professional drivers will not give up control of the keyboard. This makes the navigator feel disjointed, out of the loop, or unimportant. The problem is even worse when professional drivers seem to be unwilling to listen very much (or at all) to the navigator. This is a serious breakdown and jeopardizes the success of the pairing.

It can also be the case that the navigator may feel uncomfortable driving and has become a professional navigator. Usually this is a lack of confidence in one or more of his or her own "driving" skills.

Sometimes a person becomes a "good" professional driver because it is genuinely in the best interest of the pair and the team. His or her partner may be an extremely slow typist or have RSI (like Martin Griss in Chapter 12 on expert-expert pairs) or some other handicap. The good professional driver will willingly interact with the navigator, and the pairing can work quite well.

Another beneficial professional driving pattern can legitimately occur, but only temporarily. If you are close to a critical deadline, you may not have time for the navigator to learn a new development tool.

Refactored Solution

In the Personal Scenarios that follow we discuss many different means (sometimes highly physical) to get the keyboard away from the driver. However, the best solution is to help the professional driver learn to give up control—to help the driver learn to be a navigator. This can be unbelievably difficult because the driver may be a control freak or feel insecure without the keyboard. He or she may not have the patience required to sit back and watch a less-skilled programmer at work. The best solution might be to have the professional driver watch a good navigator working with a partner, see the interactions, and hopefully learn how pair programming must be done. Unfortunately, if the professional driver can not be trained, then it is probably best to not use that person in a pair programming situation.

In the case of professional navigators, they must force themselves to take control and do some driving so they can improve their skill sets. If that doesn't happen, the "innocent" professional driver should insist that turns be taken. Naturally, the good professional driver will willingly give up the controls and try to help the navigator become more skilled.

If you see yourself as a professional driver or a professional navigator, get over it!

The driver compensating for a handicap of his or her partner does not need to refactor the solution. Indeed, by being a professional driver, the programmer can help the navigator achieve more than ever before. Laurie remembers a brilliant student at the University of Utah who had a horrible car accident and lost motor skills in his hands. He had braces put on his arms that let him type one letter at a time, with great difficulty. His partner benefited greatly from the pairing because of the navigator's brilliant mind. The navigator benefited because he was able to use this brilliant mind without being physically hampered. Together they were a winning pair in every way.

Personal Scenarios

Interestingly, several of our survey respondents admitted to being a professional driver. To protect them, we have not included their names. We even had one respondent admit that he was a slow typist and preferred to work with a professional driver. Here are some of the respondent's comments:

> I haven't had experience with professional drivers, but maybe people who have worked with me might complain about it.

> Oh! Oh, you are talking about me! I can do that sometimes especially with an introvert or someone that doesn't type fast enough or isn't accustomed to the development environment. We just aren't moving fast enough sometimes, and it can be frustrating.

As you might imagine, some respondents claimed that it never happened to them because they were just too tough. We particularly liked what Ron Jeffries of ObjectMentor had to say:

> Nobody screws with me. I'm the XP Hammer.

However, professional driving is a very serious problem for pair programming as described in the following from a professional programmer who wishes to remain anonymous:

> I paired with an application "hero" who was the recognized expert in the application. I was the average one. He drove all of the time and was an extremely fast typist. I spent most of my time looking over his shoulder and watching him program. Most of the time he was completely silent. Fortunately, I am an experienced developer, so I could recognize most of what he was doing. Unfortunately, without his commentary, I was so wrapped up in keeping up with understanding his code that I never had a chance to contribute to the design of the code. Whenever I asked about his design, the answers were terse and sometimes monosyllabic.

Stephanie Ward of Interliant describes how drivers may actually exhibit some "hermit" characteristics:

> This is a very difficult problem to solve. I once worked with a driver where we always worked at his machine. He always drove, and therefore his ideas were always tried first when there was a disagreement. He liked to discuss an idea/implementa-

tion first and plot out the roadmap of how to proceed, but when it came time actually to code the solution, he would have been happier coding alone.

Finally, Jeff Canna of RoleModel Software states that professional drivers are just lousy partners—period:

> I've never had a problem with this as long as the driver who wouldn't give up was listening to me. The time I've had an issue with this is when the person who "needs" to drive is ignoring me; being the passenger in this case gets really old really fast. I've also found if people are insistent drivers, they tend not to be a good pair, and I do not like pairing with them.

We had many suggestions on how to solve the problem of the professional driver. Some as, mentioned earlier, simply gave up on the partner. Tim Mackinnon of Connextra says:

> This is incredibly boring; it's like watching paint dry. You don't learn the same as if you grab the keyboard. We watch for this and instruct such people to work on relinquishing control. The flip side of this is that sometimes someone is too timid to take control. We try and help people build confidence and also try and do outrageous things to get a reaction that causes the person to grab the keyboard.

A particularly poignant comment from professional programmer Anders Bengtsson describes how a little assertive behavior works, but sometimes you have to be aggressively assertive:

> This is a real problem, because if you pressure them to give up the keyboard, they will lose their interest and be of no help to you when you drive. I think it's important that both know how PP is supposed to work, so giving up the keyboard won't be a cause of conflict. Keywords like "let me drive" may be helpful. I have also had the keyboard snapped from my hands with an angry "you've been at the keyboard all day" yelled. It was somewhat comical, but it taught me that you have to offer the keyboard regularly, since not everyone will find it easy to ask for it.

On a (probably) less serious note, Michael Lindner of Sonus Networks comes up with a novel solution on how to help the professional driver stop driving. Naturally we do not support the notion of using ropes and other restraining devices:

Such people should not be allowed to drive. Tie their hands together and sit them down.

Finally, Markus Pfister of Itopia uses some good common sense. Make sure that your partner is drinking a lot of coffee, Mountain Dew, or some other liquid:

Everybody takes a break sometimes; grab the keyboard, and don't let it go.

"My Partner Is a Total Loser" and Other Excess Ego Problems

Team (*gathered around the espresso machine chatting*)

Fred (*looking down the hall at Barney*): Loser!

Rest of team (*totally shocked*)

Barney (*speaking softly*): Hey, Fred, time to get back at it.

Fred (*doesn't respond, walks to their station, sits down as the driver, starts typing*): Mutter, mutter, mutter.

Barney (*pointing*): You can't use that class; it doesn't have the correct iterator type.

Fred (*impatiently ignores Barney*): Mutter, mutter.

Barney (*pointing again*): Hey, the static function should be used instead of building that data yourself.

Fred (*more impatient, keeps ignoring Barney*): Mutter, mutter.

Barney (*looking disgusted*): Fred, your pants are on fire.

Fred (*completely blocking him out*): Mutter, mutter.

Barney (*looking amused*): Fred, an alien spacecraft just landed out in the parking lot.

Fred (*concentrating furiously*): Mutter, mutter.

Root Causes

Usually some kind of attitude problem. Often it has nothing to do with the partner; the person just feels that he or she is better than anyone else.

General Form

Recognizing this problem is sometimes quite easy. When the partner comes stomping away from the station, screaming that he or she will never pair again, you should have a pretty good indication that there is a problem. (*Note: Smoke, fire, and yelling are other good indications.*) A little digging and you will certainly uncover that one of the partners has an excess ego problem. Sometimes the person with the excess ego intimidates his or her partner so much that it is more difficult to spot. Or if the partner has some tendency toward being introverted, again it may be difficult to discern. However, switching partners will eventually lead to someone who "just can't take it anymore" and the ego issue will be found out.

Finally, we are reminded of the management technique, "Management by Walking Around" (MBWA) and its sibling "Management by Walking Around and Listening." MBWA is a more open technique where the manager frequently wanders around, talking with the team members, encouraging them, offering advice, and so on. (Note: One has to be careful not to overdo MBWA as it could come off as being overbearing, micromanaging, or "too much in your face.") The manager who is using MBWA should be able to spot the excess ego problem after observing the pair working. Observing the interactions, watching the body language, and in general interpreting how well the pair is pairing should help to tip off the manager that there is a problem.

Refactored Solution

Clearly this is a serious issue and must be dealt with as quickly as possible. The psyche and cohesion of the entire team are at risk. An amazing number of people in the Personal Scenarios indicate that they have no tolerance for the excess ego problem, and the best solution is to fire the individual. Excess ego is not to be tolerated. We have heard of people who try to solve this problem by pairing the egomaniac with someone who is definitely far superior. The hope is that it will help cut down the person's ego and provide some humility. Usually this doesn't work as the person often has the mindset: "Well, he was great, but the rest of them are losers!!" Another technique is to go through several pairings with known, good partners and show how valuable pair programming is and how effective it can be. The hope is that the egomaniac will see the benefit and learn that all partners can contribute to a successful pairing. Again, sometimes this works for a while, but as soon as the individual is paired with someone he or she needs to teach or work with, the old egomaniac issues surface, and the problem is back.

Counseling and working with and teaching the individual to keep his or her ego in check can be effective. As with many other problems, one of the most important issues is for the individual to admit that there indeed is a problem. Then, the person has to work harder when pairing to keep his or her own ego in check and learn to work with the partner no matter what the partner's particular skill level may be. This can work, but it takes an individual who can exhibit self-control and who wants to improve.

Alas, however, there may be no constructive way to solve the problem. You may be forced to relegate the person to doing individual programming tasks (although this does have the downside that unless the individual is producing code that is not used by anyone else, the person will eventually be interacting with other team members and his or her bad attitude would likely still cause problems). If that does not work then the individual is just going to have to leave.

Personal Scenarios

Professional programmer Norman Rekitt observes that attitude is an important key to successful pair programming:

> It is a fight with this one. Attitide is everything.

We concur and add that we believe that attitude is in general important for pretty much all things related to being a successful member of any software development project. Consultant Wayne Conrad, who confesses that he has egomaniac tendencies, offers the advice that if you recognize your problems, you can overcome them and create a happy, effective pairing:

> My ego makes me take control when pairing, whether I'm in the front or in the back. That makes pairing a difficult exercise in humility.

Omnigon International's Peter Merel also offers some advice on how to correct the problem of excess ego:

> Some folk just aren't cut out for development teams. In particular, I worked with one fellow who became politically active whenever he worked with others—just downright antisocial toward them. His skills weren't awful, but he was a habitual team-wrecker. There was no way to cut him from the team, so we simply let him sit in his own little world, and we developed around him. Most folks with ego problems, however, are reachable. The best way is to get them to see pairing as a goal, something for which to demonstrate prowess. If you can do that, then they work to boost their egos by getting good at it.

Several described what eventually happened to the egomaniacs. Most, as you can see, were eliminated from their positions, in one way or another. Eric Herman offers the sage advice that the manager and team members have to weigh the value of a person to a team in the face of such shortcomings:

> Most of the time, this isn't an issue. When it is, consider if the person or people are as important as they think they are. Would the team be better off without them?

"My Partner Is SO Smart" and Other Too Little Ego Problems

Patty *(settling in as the driver at the keyboard)*: Well, Pete, let's work on completing the new agent code.

Pete *(walks in and immediately falls to the ground groveling)*: I am not worthy.

Patty *(peering at Pete)*: Huh?

Pete (speaking softly): I am not worthy of being with "Patty, The Great Hacker."

Patty (ignoring him): First we'll create a class to handle the agent-to-agent interaction (she types new line).

Pete (gets up and moves into the navigator chair, looking in total awe): That was magnificent!

Patty (looking over her shoulder): What?

Pete (still in awe): Your typing skills are just marvelous. You pushed newline with such authority.

Patty (looking confused, gets back to work. She now types: `Class Conversation`.)

Pete (beaming): Wow. That was fantastic. I never would have thought of using the name "conversation."

Patty (looking unbelievingly, mutters to herself): This is going to be a very long session.

Root Causes

This seems to happen when someone simply has zero confidence in his or her own skill and feels inadequate in accomplishing even the most basic task. Often it is even worse when paired with someone with better skills.

General Form

This ego problem is often readily apparent. Nearly any partner who pairs with the individual will most likely notice it immediately and will be able to report it to the manager. In addition, any manager who observes the pair at work will certainly be able to pick up on the issue. It is also true that this problem can be more subtle. People who seriously lack confidence have often learned techniques to hide it; they are often exceedingly quiet. When they're questioned, they use techniques to turn the conversation around so they are asking the questions and trying to get opinions from others.

Refactored Solution

Clearly there are deep psychological issues that would have to be overcome in the most severe cases. However, for the remainder, there are several possible solutions. One of the keys is to let the person who lacks confidence drive. Since the driver has a very focused task to complete, it forces the person without good self-confidence to be much more active. Pairing that person with a partner who has good people skills will also be a great benefit. The navigator can work to complement the driver for each good idea and good execution of their task. This will help build up his or her confidence and self-esteem. The key is to make sure that the complements are not overdone and they are true and genuine. Overdoing the compliments is disingenuous and certainly can make the task of helping the person improve his or her self-confidence even more difficult.

When the person with low confidence is the navigator, again, the partner can work to help overcome the problem. As the team is working, if one partner is not interacting, the other can work to draw him or her out by asking questions and asking for advice. Another good technique is to introduce as much comedy and mirth as possible. Try to lighten up the situation and make the other person feel comfortable. Tell a joke (not a stupid joke, unless it is so stupid that it is funny). Make fun of the program; talk about one funny thing that happened the day before. Eventually the communication will increase, which ultimately will lead you down the path toward a better working relationship and getting your partner to open up and instill more self-confidence. Clearly it takes patience, but the reward can be a vastly improved colleague. It is also the case that not anyone can take on the role of mentor, teacher, and advisor. It takes someone with the right people skills and a high level of self-confidence.

One problem that can surface is team members feeling that the "lack of ego" person is not pulling his or her weight. This can cause heartaches for the rest of the team. They may perceive that since one person isn't working as hard as the rest, why should they be pulling all-nighters and putting in the long hours. This can be an infectious problem and clearly must be addressed.

Another problem that could arise is "flipping the bozo bit." The expression was first coined by Jim McCarthy (1995) who discusses the issue of a person or group of people who consider a colleague to be worthless and therefore a "bozo." They "flip the bozo bit," which means that the person is considered a bozo and from then on should be ignored. The bit can never be reset, and one hopes that the person doesn't screw up the rest of the team's efforts. As you might imagine, this is a very bad situation and must be solved, hopefully before it happens. It is our experience that once the bit is flipped, people will not flip it back, and the low-ego person probably should move to a different group or position.

Personal Scenarios

The most commonly offered solution to the problem of someone with a lack of self-confidence is to let that person drive. Object Mentor's Ron Jeffries states that driving is important and adds that one partner should work to get the other, low-ego partner involved:

> Low-ego partners can sit quietly and not follow. It's important to encourage them to speak and to give the "smart" person some encouragement to draw them in . . . probably should let them drive.

Inpath Solutions' Todd Jonker shows how important it is for the partner to work with low-ego people to help them improve:

> I tend to be on the receiving end of this (blush). I try to encourage my partner to ask lots of questions. I try to make him drive whenever he seems comfortable with the current work, and sometimes when he is uncomfortable, so he can have the boost of succeeding at tricky bits.

Consultant Wayne Conrad supports the notion that the partner can really help make the pairing work by asking lots of questions:

> I get this with some of my partners who just give up and stop contributing. I like to ask them little questions all the time to keep them involved. "What's a good name for that variable?" If my partner has given up, I ask him some of these little questions and accept without question any answer that's even slightly good. If I were to counter every suggestion with what I think is a slightly better idea, he'd continue to feel small. But if I let him feel in control and feel like he's improving the code, it can help to get him off the defensive and back to being involved.

Dave Chaplin of Byte-Vision Ltd. again supports the notion that the partner can help the low-ego person to succeed and offers some sage advice for those who think that they are "so smart":

> There is nothing wrong with this provided the "too smart" person is aware of this and encourages creativity from the "Too Little Ego." Modesty helps in this case with the 'so smart' pair. There is no such thing as "so smart." I like to remind people on the team that no one is a genius—he just knows a great deal about a very, very small subject.

Professional programmer Iain Lowe points out some of the difficulties of working with someone who has a lack of ego:

> I have worked with one individual who makes it hard to do things because she refuses to believe in what her own head tells her. She needed me to confirm every step she made. I found this made for very slow going.

We must say that we wholeheartedly agree with John Sisk of RADSoft who really hits the issue home with his statement about what pair programming is all about:

> Easy to assume that you are dumb and everyone else is smart. But in pair programming everyone has something to contribute, and nobody knows it all.

References

McCarthy, J. (1995). *Dynamics of Software Development*, Microsoft Press.

Case Studies of Pair Programming in a Software Process

We believe that pair programming is a highly versatile technique. It is valuable in a broad range of contexts and can be a part of any software development process. It can also be used by some or all of the members of a project team.

Part Four will examine two software development processes in which pair programming is an integral part. In Chapter 26, we'll look at the Extreme Programming methodology and its use of pair programming. In Chapter 27, we'll look at the Collaborative Software Process, the process Laurie developed in her pair programming research. The message we want to send is that pairing can fit into any software development methodology (or could even be used by programmers who operate without any form of methodology) as a means for obtaining all the different benefits we've discussed so far.

Pair Programming in a Software Process Case Study: Extreme Programming (XP)

This chapter describes a disciplined, agile software development methodology, Extreme Programming (XP) (Auer and Miller 2001, Beck 2000, Beck and Fowler 2001, Jeffries et al. 2001). After describing XP, we'll give our views on why pair programming is an integral part of realizing success with an XP project.

A Life-Cyle Evolution

In the evolution of software development methodologies, first came the code-and-fix model. People were simply using computers to "find the answer," to perform computation that took too long to do "by hand."For this type of development, code-and-fix was fine. (The fact that is it still in wide use today is worrisome, though.) Code-and-fix can be classified as ad hoc, meaning that the methods used are tailored to the situation or problem at hand and are not necessarily applicable to any other situation or problem.

Then came the waterfall process. This process was first published in 1970 by Winton Royce. Royce broke the software development process into five steps: requirements definition, system and software design, implementation and unit testing, integration and system testing, and operation and maintenance. A key to the waterfall process is that a step had to be done perfectly because once a step was done, it was never revisited. All future development used the artifacts of previous steps without looking back. Many organizations have graduated from code-and-fix to the waterfall model. However, current thinking says the "never look back" policy is not advisable, especially when requirements are rapidly changing. (Actually, Royce's original work did have feedback loops to earlier steps. A simplification of his model ultimately became the legendary waterfall model.)

The shortcomings of the waterfall model motivated the spiral model. In 1988, Boehm proposed the spiral development model, which essentially said that the first two steps of the waterfall model (requirements definition and system and software design) would still be done for the whole project. Then the next two (implementation and unit testing and integration and system testing) would be done iteratively. That is, the programmers would be assigned pieces of the designed system and would work on the implementation, integration, and testing for that piece. When that piece was integrated and tested, the programmers would be assigned another piece. This was a big improvement over the waterfall model because smaller pieces could be completed and integrated, making the process much more manageable. Certain development processes based on this model also allowed for customers to give feedback on groups of these smaller chunks of functionality, often called *increments* or *releases*. (Sometimes this led to doing the fifth step, operation and maintenance, incrementally.) Current perspectives on the spiral model are that the detailed completion of the first two steps, requirements and design, led to unresponsive projects because they did not change the project requirements or design based on any midstream customer feedback.

Along Comes XP

These shortcomings motivated the originators of XP (Kent Beck, Ward Cunningham, and Ron Jeffries) to create XP. All five of waterfall's steps are done incrementally and often. The main benefit of doing this is to be as agile as possible to requirements changes while still managing cost and schedule. We will describe XP in the context of waterfall's five steps. With XP, these five steps are done highly iterative. Developers quite often cycle several times between design, implementation, and testing in the course of an hour's work.

Requirements Definition

Requirements are gathered and scheduled employing user stories and the release planning process. To begin, customers work with developers or requirements analysts to gather requirements. This is done very informally. A customer speaks about a requirement, and the developer writes down the requirement on an index card, almost verbatim, in the customer's own language. There is no intent to specify completely the customer's requirement on the index card. The card is a commitment for future conversation between the developer and the customer. When all the cards are done, the customer is asked to prioritize these user stories (or requirements).

The developers then work with the stories. They read the stories and ask questions of an on-site customer about what is desired. From this, the developers estimate how long the story will take to implement. If a story is too big (that is, it would take longer than a week to complete), the customer is asked to break the story into smaller stories. To come up with the estimate, the developers look at how long it has taken them to complete other similar stories. They also assess the risk associated with the story.

With each story card having a description, a priority, a resource estimate, and a risk assessment, Release Planning (often known as the "Planning Game") is performed, using these cards as the playing pieces. The "game" is played by laying all the cards on the table and sliding, rearranging, and reorganizing them. The object of the game is to decide which stories get implemented in the next release, trying to maximize the number of high-priority stories. With XP, a release is generally no more than three months long, which results in a program that delivers functionality to the customer. Each release is broken into three or four iterations (a three-week period) and results in an internal development deliverable. At the end of each iteration, the team assesses the stories they have been able to complete and makes a new plan for the successful completion of the release (perhaps involving a new, smaller Release Plan to reset the Release Plan based on actual results). At the end of Release Planning, the team knows which stories will be done in the next iteration.

Developers sign up to implement the user stories. One developer is the owner of each story. All work is done in pairs and the story owner recruits a partner to work with on each subtask, based on the technical aspects of that particular subtask.

While the story is being implemented, many questions will arise. With XP, it is very important to have an on-site customer representative to clarify these requirements at any time. XP practitioners believe that many problems arise because requirements are not completely or accurately specified or because the developers simply don't understand the requirement. An on-site customer can clarify the requirements, which will prevent the developer from having to make many assumptions on what the customer probably wanted.

Another important job of the on-site customer is to work with the developers to create acceptance (or functional) test cases. They define what kinds of things they want to see the system do in order to feel assured that a user story has been properly implemented. In developing these test cases, the customer also clarifies his or her requirements.

In traditional development, the customer and the requirements analysts work to define a detailed, consistent, correct, and verifiable document that describes what the customer wants. This becomes a contract of what needs to be delivered. Conversely, with XP the developers do not seek to understand requirements completely until they really need to. They gain this understanding in real time by talking to the customer (discussions over documents) and by reviewing acceptance test cases. In this way the customer and the developer gain understanding of desirable functionality later in the process—once they both have more knowledge of the capabilities of the current system and of the domain/problem to be solved.

Once a release has been completed and delivered to the customer, Release Planning is redone to determine which user stories will be implemented in the next release. At this time the customer has ample opportunity to change the priorities and the stories themselves.

System and Software Design

XP does not produce big design documents before getting started. XP'ers call this BDUF for "big design up front" and believe that the development of these documents is not cost-effective. The idea here is that software engineers change their minds about how they will implement something once they try it and once they get feedback on completed work. If you skip the documentation step, you will start producing software assets that have value to your customer, not just to your documents. Surely there will be rework and refactoring because of the lack of up-front design, but there will be less time spent reworking and refactoring than would have gone into the BDUF. In addition, you will have assets, not paper. After a release is completed, some XP teams also create some bare-bones documentation that records what they *did do*, not what they *planned* to do. Of course, if the customer writes a story concerned with the need for documentation and assigns the priority of it high enough to make it into a release, documentation will be created to suit the customer's desires.

In traditional development, a system architecture is developed to provide a map of how all the pieces fit together. The closest that XP comes to that is the system metaphor. For example, in the original XP project, the C3 project was a payroll system. The metaphor that was used was an assembly line. As a paycheck went down the assembly line, it was given all the pieces of information it needed. When it got to the end of the assembly line, it had all of the necessary information. All the developers on the C3 project had the assembly-line mental model in their heads, which helped them to visualize how all the pieces fit together. "The metaphor gives the team a consistent picture they can use to describe the way the existing system works, where new parts fit, and what form they should take" (Auer and Miller 2001).

In general, when a pair starts to work on a story, they read the story and do whatever they need to do to feel comfortable that they can handle it. This may be an impromptu CRC card session (Beck and Cunningham 1989, Bellin and Simone 1997), or it may be to write down a quick diagram on a white board. The pair uses any tools and technique that any other software developer might use to devise a design; however, they use only what they feel is necessary to tackle the task at hand. The artifacts of this process—the notes, cards, and diagrams—are never officially archived for future use. Once the pair feels comfortable that they have a good view of their direction, they begin to code.

A very important part of XP's design philosophy is "do the simplest thing that could possibly work" and the "You Aren't Gonna Need It" (YAGNI) philosophy. The XP premises emphasize sticking to the user story at hand. Doing anything else is speculative, at best, and requires us to assume we know what the customer wants. These XP premises run counter to traditional software engineering doctrine concerning the Cost of Change curve (Boehm 1981). The traditional Cost of Change curve indicates that the later change enters the development cycle, the exponentially more expensive it is. XP proponents contend that its practices flatten the Cost of Change curve (Beck 2000) and that late change is not (much) more expensive. The time saved by not producing BDUF and plans is more than the required rework to handle change later in the development cycle.

The last thing to mention, as far as XP design goes, is refactoring, the technique of improving code without changing its functionality. Martin Fowler has championed this technique (Fowler et al. 1999). The first pass on the code is to do the simplest thing that could possibly work to get the user story running. Then pairs refactor in the process of implementing more functionality, or there is an explicit, deliberate time where the pair refactors code in order to improve the design of their working, functional implementation.

Code Implementation and Unit Testing

Before the pair writes a single line of production code, they write their first automated unit test case. The programmer cycles through tight "create a few test cases"/"write a bit of code" cycles. In object-oriented code, this means they write unit tests for every method they plan to implement. These tests show that the method works as intended and handles error conditions gracefully. Naturally, since the code has not been written, these test cases will initially fail. The pair then writes just enough code to make these test cases succeed. As more and more functionality is properly implemented, more and more test cases will pass. The job is not done until both the functionality for the user story is completed, and 100 percent of the unit tests are successful. One hundred percent of the unit test cases that were ever written for the entire product must also pass. Only then can the developer know that the new functionality was successfully implemented without breaking anything else in the project.

The entire development team owns the entire code base (called "Collective Code Ownership"). This means that any pair can change any line of code in the entire code base in order to add functionality or to refactor. The pair does not need to ask permission of the author of that section. They just have to make sure that all the unit tests ever written on the code base still run successfully.

Last, because of pair programming and collective code ownership, each XP project has commenting guidelines and follows a coding standard. This is necessary because everyone on the team needs to be able to understand anyone else's code to enhance it or refactor it quickly. However, the commenting emphasis is to have self-documenting or self-revealing code rather than too many comments (which might become out-of-date or obsolete).

A common trend in modern software development is to integrate often. XP practices "Continuous Integration," whereby pairs put new functionality (code changes and the newly written unit test cases) under source control in the code base as soon as all the unit test cases pass. This happens at the end of every pairing session. The pair will have run 100 percent of the unit test cases for the system, and all of them will have passed before integration.

Acceptance Testing

Acceptance testing is done using the test cases developed and agreed on by the customer. These tests are used to measure the progress of system development (in terms of either the absolute number or the percentage of test cases that pass). They make a statement of how much functionality has been properly implemented in the system. It is always good to automate these tests, too, so that it is easy to tell if any new functionality breaks any functional test cases that had previously passed.

XP Needs Pair Programming

We believe pair programming is an integral part of XP, and it is dangerous to do XP without doing pair programming. One primary reason is that the pairs keep each other honest. XP is a minimalist approach, so it is essential that many of the practices actually get done. The various practices have checks and balances on each other. Alistair Cockburn classifies XP as a "high discipline" process because it is very important that the developers follow the practices, however minimal they are. In *Agile Software Development* (2001), Cockburn says the following about XP:

[It] is a high-discipline methodology . . . it calls for tight adherence to strict coding and design standards, very strong unit test suites that must pass at all times, good acceptance tests, constant work in pairs, vigilance in keeping the design simple, and aggressive refactoring. . . . It turns out that most people *like* working in pairs. Programming in pairs plays to their pride in work, since they get more done in less time, with fewer errors, and usually end up with a better design. They like this. As a result, they program in pairs voluntarily. While in pairs, they encourage each other to follow coding standards and write tests so the discipline is kept in place by the paired programming.

In this respect, pair programming is highly beneficial because the pair-pressure aspects of pairing cause people to be more likely actually to follow the practices. If developers don't really feel like writing good unit test cases, they might do it anyway because they are too embarrassed to skip them with their partner watching. Navigators can also identify problems with coding standards and comments. Drivers are much more likely to ensure the code is, indeed, simple and self-documenting, lest they fear the perpetual navigator question, "Can you tell me what you are doing?"

Last, since no formal design is ever done, it is wonderful for the pair to devise the design on-the-fly together—an impromptu CRC card session, perhaps? Together, they are assured of producing a better design than either could have produced alone.

References

Auer, K. and Miller, R. (2002). *Extreme Programming Applied: Playing to Win.* Addison-Wesley.

Beck, L. and Cunningham, W. (1989) "A Laboratory for Teaching Object-Oriented Thinking," Proceedings of SIGPLAN OOPSLA, October 1989.

Beck, K. (2000). *Extreme Programming Explained: Embrace Change*, Addison-Wesley.

Beck, K. and Fowler, M. (2001). *Planning Extreme Programming*, Addison-Wesley.

Bellin, D. and Simone, S. S. (1997). *The CRC Card Book*, Addison-Wesley.

Boehm, B. (1981). *Software Engineering Economics*, Prentice Hall.

Boehm, B. (1988). "A Spiral Model for Software Development and Enhancement," *IEEE Computer*, Vol. 21 (5), May 1988, pp. 61–72.

Cockburn, A. (2002). *Agile Software Development*, Addison-Wesley.

Fowler, M., Beck, K., Brant, J., Opdyke, W., and Roberts, D. (1999). *Refactoring: Improving the Design of Existing Code*, Addison-Wesley.

Jeffries, R., Anderson, A., and Hendrickson, C. (2001). *Extreme Programming Installed*, Addison-Wesley.

Newkirk, J. W. and Martin, R. C. (2001). *Extreme Programming in Practice*, Addison-Wesley.

Royce, W. W. (1970). "Managing the Development of Large Software Systems: Concepts and Techniques," *IEEE WESTCON*, Los Angeles, Ch. 3.

Succi, G. and Marchesi, M. , Eds. (2001). *Extreme Programming Examined*, Addison-Wesley.

Wake, W. C. (2002). *Extreme Programming Explored*, Addison-Wesley.

Pair Programming in a Software Process Case Study: Collaborative Software Process (CSP)

The previous chapter described an agile software development methodology, Extreme Programming (XP). Now we will briefly describe another methodology, the Collaborative Software Process (CSP). CSP is a process specifically designed to leverage the power of pair programmers. Elements of CSP have been taken from XP (Auer and Miller 2001; Beck 2000; Jeffries et al. 2001) and from Watts Humphrey's Personal Software Process (PSP) (1995). Laurie created the CSP and documented it in her dissertation (2000).

The purpose of this chapter is two-fold. Most important, it is to show that almost any proven process can be adapted to incorporate pair programing. The process can realize all the benefits of pair programming (higher quality, reduced cycle time, and so on) to make it even better. Mark Paulk of the SEI reflects on the ability of pair programming to fulfill the CMM Level 3 requirement of peer reviews, "Pair programming addresses peer reviews and is arguably more powerful than many peer review techniques because it adopts preventive concepts found in code reading and literate programming" (2001). (Paulk also indicates that more empirical research is necessary before declaring pair programming a substitute for peer review. We agree, as we discuss in the next chapter.)

Second, the purpose of this chapter is to provide the documentation for a second process that incorporates pair programming. Humphrey specifically designed PSP so that individual software engineers had procedures to address all the key process areas of Capability Maturity Model (CMM) of the Software Engineering Institute (SEI) (Paulk et al. 1993). As a result, CSP does likewise.

In 1998, Karl Weigers published an essay, "Read My Lips: No New Process Models" (1998). He says the following:

> . . . The software industry does not need any more models right now. We don't need a lot of new formalisms for software development, new design methods, new life-cycle approaches, new frameworks for process improvement, or new quality models. . . . What we do need is for practitioners routinely and effectively to apply the techniques defined by our existing models and frameworks. Once we've reached the practical limit of these approaches, we can turn to improved models that provide guidance for working in better ways.

The purpose of this chapter is not necessarily to throw another process in the ring, but to demonstrate again how the practice of pair programming is beneficial to almost any process—to help practitioners routinely and effectively apply the techniques of pair programming in their desired process.

CSP Overview

The CSP is an extension of the PSP, and it relies on the foundation of the PSP. The CSP incorporates the evolutionary learning approach of PSP, whereby engineers implementing the CSP gradually learn to incorporate the techniques into their own process. CSP has three focus areas. New users of the CSP start at Focus Area 0, incorporate quality management techniques in Focus Area 1, and follow with project management techniques at Focus Area 2. As we describe each of these Focus Areas, we CSP with XP and PSP.

Focus Area 0: Baselining Your Process

In the CSP, work is done in pairs. In Focus Area 0, pairs of engineers continue to use their "natural" process, producing the artifacts they've typically produced. The purpose of this level is to get used to working in pairs and to provide baseline measurements that can be compared with results of future process improvements. We want to know if adding steps to our process to improve quality or productivity actually works. If it doesn't work, then why even bother? The only way really to know if we're getting better is to measure ourselves.

So engineers record how much time they spend on their tasks. They also record info about the defects they remove from their programs when they do things like reviews or testing. It's good to record this information based on the phase of the development cycle. Then you can see all kinds of interesting facts, for example, you barely spend any time in design, but you spend 75 percent of your time in test (could it be that if you had a better design you could get through test easier?). Or, you might see that when you pair program, you spend 1 percent of your time getting a clean compile, but when you program alone, you end up spending 5 percent of your time getting a clean compile. Admittedly, recording this data will feel like a hassle, but it does provide great information to help you be the best (pair) programmer you can be. It also lets you keep good historical data that you can use later to make achievable commitments so you don't overcommit yourself. Last, it will help you as you constructively interact with your boss on your past project performance and the relationship of past history to future commitments. We'll talk more about that in Focus Area 2.

PSP definitely does this software process data collection and analysis. XP doesn't really, although informal recording of the total time spent on each task is often done and used for future estimation. PSP's time-tracking procedures specify that the time spent in each development phase (design, design review, code, and so on) is recorded to the minute. CSP advocates a quick cycling through the design, code, compile, and test phases as functionality is added to the system. As a result, it is hard to record the time spent in each phase. We believe it is important to record and understand the total time spent on each task and to understand the percentage of "new development" and "rework" time. New development time is when some sort of asset—like code or tests— is being produced for the first time. Rework time is when the the quality of assets is being improved, via debugging or getting test cases to pass. So CSP focuses on tracking the total time spent, divided into new development and rework phases.

A very important thing that happens in Level 0 is engineers learn to work in pairs. Most programmers have been conditioned to work individually; switching to collaborative programming is certainly an adjustment. Many engineers venture into their first pair programming experience skeptical that they would actually benefit from collaborative work. They wonder about coordinating schedules and the added communication that will be required; about adjusting to the other's working habits, programming style, and ego; and about disagreeing on aspects of the implementation.

The adjustment period to pair programming sometimes happens instantaneously. Often it takes hours or days, depending on the individuals. A major milestone occurs when a newbie loses the instinct or the inhibition to tear the keyboard out of his or her partner's hands (depending on the partner's temperament). It also takes a while for a programmer to learn to leverage the power of the person sitting next to him or her—to know when to ask for help and to know how to accept help graciously. It also takes a while to learn how to help the driver constructively without feeling as if you are correcting or criticizing. It does not take many victorious, clean compiles or declarations of "We just got through our test with no defects!" for the teams to celebrate their union—and to feel like one jelled, collaborative team.

So, people getting started with CSP learn how to record basic time and defect information, and they learn how to work together as a pair. Next, in Focus Area 1, they learn some techniques intended to help them more predictably produce high-quality projects.

Focus Area 1: Quality Management

As we said, the engineers start to add specific techniques to improve their chances of predictably producing high-quality code. Quite possibly, the engineer's baseline process already requires him or her to do some of these techniques; then, of course, no change is required.

The first of these techniques is to understand your requirements by preparing use cases. The first step in developing the use cases is to identify the actors, the people or systems that are external to the system but act upon or with the system. Then the use cases themselves can be discovered. A use case is a sequence of transactions performed by a system that yields a measurable result of values for a particular actor. A use case typically represents major functionality that is complete from beginning to end. Each use case is iteratively explored by completing a use case flow of events. In the Flow of Events, use case preconditions and the handling of normal and alternative scenarios is documented. The Use Case Flow of Events is also useful for functional test case development. Engineers can identify many paths through the flow of events and devise test cases to validate the correctness of the program for that set of conditions. We highly recommend Alistair Cockburn's *Writing Effective Use Cases* (2000) for people learning how to write use cases.

The PSP assumes programmers have a documented set of requirements and focuses on the design and implementation of those requirements. XP has a much more informal requirements gathering technique via its user story cards, which can be compared to informal use cases (without the flow of events documentation).

Once the use cases are complete, a CRC card brainstorming exercise is held. The exercise helps discover the system's objects and their public interfaces. In a CRC card modeling session, participants identify candidate classes based on problem requirement statements. Then participants walk through various scenarios (which can be found on the use case flow of events) in order to determine what services each class needs to provide (its responsibilities) and what information the class needs to know (its attributes). The walkthrough also identifies which other classes a class is dependent on for services or information (its collaborators). These responsibilities, attributes, and collaborators are recorded on index cards.

PSP does not advocate any particular way of discovering classes. Extreme Programmers don't always do CRC cards, but a pair might kick off an impromptu CRC card session at any time to help them get started on a design for a user story.

CSP also focuses on writing unit tests and black box, or functional, tests. Black box/functional test cases are written early—in the design stage, or even earlier, in the requirements analysis stage. The philosophy behind this is that if you diabolically think about "how can I break this code" and write test cases to see if you have or not, you will design and code in order to pass the test cases. Writing and reviewing these test cases can also help you understand your requirements or cause you to ask customers questions so you can understand them. An often ignored, but very important, reason to write test cases early is that when a project is in the chaotic throes of testing with a deadline looming, the development of a complete set of test cases is often compromised and/or not done. The lack of a thorough set of test cases can have a debilitating effect on the quality of a software project.

PSPers write test cases, but not until after code has been written. In most software development processes, engineers author a contractual requirements specification. In comparison, XP developers work with customers to develop high-level acceptance test cases, which certainly helps to clarify requirements. When these test cases run successfully, the User Story is deemed contractually satisfied.

Another practice of CSP to improve quality is to create incrementally an extensive, automated set of white box test cases. A small chunk of functionality is chosen for implementation. Test cases are written for this chunk before code is written. Then code is written, and the test cases (and all the other test cases that were ever written on the code) are run. The new code is done when all the test cases are passed. This iterative process of "design-a-little, write-some-test cases, code-a-little, test-a-little" allows development to proceed with confidence that the code is correct. It also improves defect removal efficiency because if a test case fails, the engineer can be assured that the new code caused the fault.

Again, PSPers write test cases, but not until after code has been written. CSP adopted XP's unit testing techniques and philosophy.

The last CSP technique for focusing on quality is the analysis of measurements. As we said in Focus Area 0, engineers started recording information about the time they spent and the defects they removed. Now this data is turned into significantly more information in order to provide measurement-based feedback. By analyzing the measurements, engineers can learn about how they work. For example, they can see

- The percentage of time they spend in new development versus rework phases.

- Where they remove most of their defects. If they are removing syntax defects in the compile phase, is the navigator daydreaming or asleep on the job?

- What kinds of defects they remove during functional test. If they have many functional test defects, how can they adjust their pair process so this doesn't happen anymore?

- Where in the process they are most error prone. How can they adjust their process to be less error prone and more careful during this phase?

- How these measurements change as they start introducing the practices outlined in this focus area (use cases, CRC cards, testing, and so on). If they start a practice and don't notice any improvement, maybe they don't need to do that practice, or they need to do a better job incorporating that practice.

This information can provide critical feedback so engineers can effectively critique their own work and adjust their pair process. If you start engraining some of these quality practices into your methodology, you should see fewer defects in your code, and you will spend more time in new development phases and less time in rework phases.

XP doesn't collect these quality metrics. CSP inherits these metrics and the measurement-based feedback philosophy from PSP.

Once the programmers have learned that these practices are meant to improve their quality, they can start to focus on making their schedule more accurate and predictable.

Focus Area 2: Project Management

CSP practitioners add to their process techniques that will help them manage their time and make and keep commitments. CSP is an interactive development process. Iterations should be no longer than three to four weeks. You want to have something to show at the end of each iteration, something that works, something you can get external feedback on. If you spend too much time only on internal workings of the project, you're sure to get some changes to these internals as soon as you start implementing stuff that works with it. You need to do something that will be viewed as progress by the most skeptical customer. You need to pass some functional test cases, similar to the measure of progess in XP.

These short iterations have two purposes. First, it is great to have customers take a look at each iteration and to give feedback on whether the project is doing what they want it to do. Maybe you're not doing exactly what the customers thought you'd do. Maybe they tried out what you did and that gave them a great idea or made them realize they didn't really want what they thought they wanted. Maybe their priorities have changed. The main thing to realize is that we have trouble understanding perfectly what our customers want and that sometimes our customers don't know exactly what they want. No amount of planning or documenting can change that. We need to be able to react to customer changes as well as to our own improved understanding of the system. Software development processes that strive to be able to react to these inevitable changes are classified as agile or adaptive; we consider CSP an agile process.

Second, shorter iterations also help to set boundaries on the accuracy and scope of detailed planning. The law of diminishing returns definitely applies to detailed project planning. You can probably plan what you can accomplish today pretty well. You can probably also plan what you could accomplish this week. Beyond that, it gets fuzzy. It's hard to know what you can do next week without knowing what you did this week. Maybe things went faster or more slowly than you had planned.

Project management is generally started by making a rough resource estimate for the project by first reviewing the problem statement and a conceptual design. This estimate is used to determine if the scope and the budget are even in the ballpark. At this point, a "go/no-go" decision needs to be made if the budget, the scope, and the schedule simply cannot be reconciled. However, some win-win negotiating tactics need to come into play before a "no-go" decision is made. Phases such as, "We can't finish it by then, but we can get you all but x by then" or "What's the minimum functionality you need to launch your product?" should be heard.

So, assuming the project is a go, activities such as use cases and CRC cards are done to help understand and document the customer requirements and to break the project into one- to three-week activities that different developers can own. At this point, you might be wondering if, with pair programming, one or two developers own the activities. Individual developers "own" their own activities. Other programmers rotate around the team to help complete these activities. Generally, the activities are broken into small (half-day or full-day) tasks. It is most beneficial when team members pair with other members when a particular task touches parts of the system they are both knowledgeable in or they both should be knowledgeable in.

So, the project requirements are understood and the activities are assigned. Now we need to have the activity owners estimate how long it will take to complete their assignments. For this estimation they have two valuable resources to tap: past records and each other. First, let's look at the records they have. All the way back in the Focus Area 0, they should have started recording how much time they spent on our tasks. This data is invaluable when we need to develop new estimates for how long things will take us. Ideally, we can look through all the activities of the current or past projects and see who did them and how long the tasks actually took. Then we can think about how different or similar our current activities are, based on our estimates of our past. When we're estimating, it's also really important to talk to each other. If you look at the list of past activities and find one that's pretty similar, talk to the people who did it. Find out what difficulties they had and what advice they can share with you on your estimate.

Now all the manageable pieces of the iteration, the activities, have been estimated and have owners. You break these activities down into the smallest measurable unit in project management, the task. Tasks should be able to be done in a half day or a full day. They are things that you can "check off" often. You might pair with a different person for each task, depending on which parts of the system that particular task touches. You break down your activities for the iteration into these tasks. Project progress measures the percentage of these tasks you accomplish. Using a PSP term, we call this step measuring the *earned value*. You earn the value of a task by completing it.

Laurie visited an organization that made only one change to their prior development process: to break their project planning into weekly activities and then into daily tasks. By doing this, the engineers assumed much more responsibility and ownership for completing things. It's really hard to get a firm grasp on what you have to do if you're assigned some "big thing" that you have six months to finish. You "go for the checkmark" if you have short, measurable tasks, especially if, once you complete the tasks, you can pass a test case that you couldn't pass before.

CSP's project management approach is truly a hybrid of both PSP and XP. The short iterations and task planning are very similar to XP. Basing future estimates on history is advocated by both methodologies, although PSP's method of extrapolating new estimates from history is based on a fairly complicated proxy-based approach involving linear regression. As we said, CSP used PSP's earned value tracking in order to determine what percentage of a project or increment has been completed.

Summary

CSP was adapted from PSP. The PSP was developed to guide a singular software engineer in how to produce high-quality software predictably and to provide mechanisms for measurement-based feedback and analysis. This singular engineer could be an island in the middle of a sea of hackers or could be on a team of PSP practitioners, because the PSP does not create any specific dependencies between programmers and the process they use. CSP is similar: Any pair of developers could choose to follow the CSP regardless of whether the rest of their team does. Part of the reason that PSP and CSP can be so "pluggable" is because neither process considers team coordination and projectwide architecture kinds of things. These are covered in a team structure such as that outlined in Watts Humphrey's Team Software Process (TSP) (2000). With TSP, team members assume roles (such as team leader, quality manager, planning manager, development manager) and complete specific documents to aid in team communication. Software developers following PSP or CSP can work together on a team that uses the TSP.

References

Auer, K. and Miller, R. (2001). *Extreme Programming Applied: Playing to Win*, Addison-Wesley.

Beck, K. (2000). *Extreme Programming Explained: Embrace Change*, Addison-Wesley.

Cockburn, A. (2001). *Writing Effective Use Cases*, Addison-Wesley.

Humphrey, W. S. (1995). *A Discipline for Software Engineering*, Addison-Wesley.

Humphrey, W. S. (2000). *Introduction to the Team Software Process*, Addison-Wesley.

Jeffries, R., Anderson, A., and Hendrickson, C. (2001). *Extreme Programming Installed*, Addison-Wesley.

Paulk, M. C. , Curtis, B. , and Chrisis, M. B. (1993). "Capability Maturity Model for Software Version 1. 1." *CMU/SEI-93-TR*, Software Engineering Institute.

Paulk, M. "Extreme Programming from a CMM Perspective," *IEEE Software*, Vol. 18, No. 6, November/December 2001.

Wiegers, K. (1998) *Read My Lips: No New Models!* IEEE Software, Vol. 15, No. 5, September/October 1998.

Williams, L. A. (2000). "The Collaborative Software Process," Ph. D. dissertation, University of Utah.

In Closing

You've taken a journey with us. Part One gave us an understanding of the practice of pair programming and how it can be viewed from several different perspectives. Part Two discussed more tactical implementation issues. In Part Three, we entertained and informed you about the various combinations of pairs and when it is best to use each kind of pair. In Part Four, we put pair programming into the context of two different software development processes.

We complete the book with Part Five. Chapter 26 discusses several different and emerging ways to expand the pair programming model beyond two colocated programmers working at one computer. And in Chapter 27, we close with Seven Habits of Effective Pair Programmers.

Moving Ahead, Going Beyond

Today, many colocated professional programmers are practicing pair programming. There are, however, some alternatives and variations emerging that can increase the scope and influence beyond two developers passing the keyboard back and forth. Some of these will be discussed in this chapter.

Triplets

Often, we've heard "two's company, three's a crowd" or "the third wheel" when we've asked people about triplet programming. But then we've also heard some success stories. The success stories had two common and simultaneous requisites: three very experienced, very mature, very responsible developers, and complex problems that can justify three brains. With these components, triplet programming can be a route to a solution to a very tough problem.

Jim Coplien tells of an effective triplet at Bell Labs: one person at the keyboard, one at the white board, and the last "thinking out loud," representing the customer (Coplien 2002). (Maybe the third could even be a real customer.) The third person can think without losing any brainpower to using his or her hands.

Multidisciplinary Pairs

The pairs don't need to be comprised of two code developers. In the scenario in the first chapter, the privacy expert paired with the Web form designer, ensuring that the forms did not violate any privacy policies. User interface specialists or Web page artists/designers can pair with programmers. (After all, some of us who were given the ability to program were slighted in the artistic part of the brain.) Jim Coplien reports, "At Mediagenix, a tester sometimes pairs with a developer as the tester drives with tests, and the developer fixes bugs. This makes it possible to circumvent the project's formal bug reporting bureaucracy, reducing the time to a stable load" (2002). Last, we've heard many reports of developers pairing with customers, which has the added advantage of real-time requirements clarification.

Code Inspections Obsolete?

Don't jump to any conclusions too fast. As we said earlier in the book, 80 percent of all programmers don't do formal code reviews. For these folks, the continual reviews of pair programming are certainly beneficial. But what can be said about groups that already do code reviews? Does pair programmed code need to be reinspected?

For over 20 years, numerous studies have documented the benefits of reviews and inspections for efficient defect removal (Fagan 1976, Russell 1991, Weller 1993). These studies need to be reexamined to determine the efficiency and effectiveness of inspection after pair programming. So, our answer right now is, "We don't know yet."

Projection Screens

In Chapter 8, we discussed the use of at least 17-inch monitors. What if we go way beyond that and project the work-in-progress on the wall? A team of researchers at the University of North Carolina, Chapel Hill, are working on the "Office of the Future" and the development of just the right technology to project programming work-in-progress. "From now on, one does not have to cramp the information into a relatively small monitor, but to have as much space as possible and to be limited only by the amount of space around" (Rascar et. al. 1998). Then the navigator will certainly have no trouble seeing the work of the driver, will likely be more alert, and can actually stand up and point to any areas of concern.

Such a setup would also be supportive of triplet programming. Jim Coplien witnessed such a programming team in action. "At Mediagenix we found teams that 'programmed with the projector' where the computer screen was projected onto a wall, and a team jointly commented and guided the work as one person sat at the keyboard" (2002).

Distributed Pair Programming

What if pairs cannot be physically next to each other? It has been established that distance does matter (Olson and Olson 2000); colocated teams perform better. Therefore it is predicted that face-to-face pair programmers will outperform distributed pair programmers in terms of sheer productivity. However, the inevitability of distributed work in contemporary software development calls for research in determining how to make this type of work most effective.

There are some initial research findings and experiences with distributed pair programming. First, we had a joint development team consisting of students from North Carolina State University, led by Laurie, and students from University of North Carolina, Chapel Hill (UNC), led by Dr. David Stotts. The students used Windows NetMeeting to work jointly on one development environment and to speak with each other using a microphone/headset. We list the following findings from this experiment:

1. At least one, but perhaps periodic, face-to-face meeting is beneficial. The students used one such meeting to get to know each other and to brainstorm their initial system architecture.

2. We purchased webcams for the students; they never felt the need to use them. We had surmised that they might periodically use them to talk to each other "face-to-face" or might draw a quick sketch of something and then hold it up to the camera. This need never arose.

3. Using a tool that allows for the distributed teams to switch quickly between a design view, such as a class diagram, and a code view is beneficial. The TogetherSoft Control Center[1] has this capability.

---

[1] See http://togethersoft.com

4. Distributed pair programmers must absolutely be willing to speak while they work. They must explain what they are doing as they are doing it, or the navigator quickly gets lost. This is so essential that programmers who are not willing to speak almost continuously should probably not try to work this way. Because of this, it is likely that the percentage of the population that can do distributed pair programming will be smaller than that that can pair program while colocated with a partner.

We will continue this research with larger sample sizes of students and with practitioners in industry. Results of a Distributed Extreme Programming experiment between Siemens developers in Germany and India (Kircher et al. 2001) yielded results similar to ours. They did, however, recommend the use of video to assess what a partner was thinking or his or her reaction to a comment or suggestion. In other contexts, we've also heard of pairs preferring pcAnywhere to NetMeeting for application sharing.

Laurie and Dr. Stotts plan to work on enhanced collaborative environments for distributed pair programmers. We propose to build a more effective collaborative environment for pair programming using the results of some simple wall-size display experiments at UNC (Bishop 2000, Bishop and Welch 2000). We will apply the principles uncovered at Bellcore in the VideoWindow project (Fish et al. 1990). In this experiment, two rooms (coffee lounges) in different buildings at Bellcore were outfitted with video cameras and wall-sized projections. In essence, an image of one lounge was sent to the other and projected on the back wall, giving the illusion in each room of a double-size coffee lounge. The researchers discovered that many users found the setup to be very natural for human communication, due to its size. Two people, one in each room, would approach the wall to converse, standing approximately the same distance from the wall that they would stand from each other in face-to-face conversations.

We believe a more effective collaborative environment can be created with a wall-sized display produced by projectors and that a corresponding improvement in distributed pair programming will result from this enhanced support for collaboration. We will mix video imagery (allowing the collaborators to see each other) with digital display information (the source code being developed). Communication will be via directional microphones placed in the vicinity of the workstations, so the participants will not be encumbered with headsets. Two distributed collaborators will interact much as they do with local pairing; to talk, one will turn to the other (face the projection wall) and speak openly in the room. Since the camera is on the projection wall, the remote collaborator will have the impression that the communicator is looking at him or her. Each will see surrounding context and an image of significant size. The illusion to be created is a "joint office" with the video walls, much like the virtual coffee lounge of Bellcore's VideoWindow.

Pair Learning

Supported by grants from the National Science Foundation, educators at North Carolina State University and at the University of California, Santa Cruz, are assessing the use of pair programming in beginning computer science classes. Through this research, they are examining whether working in a pair enhances a student's ability to learn with another beginning student. They are also examining how these students perform in later semesters when they are forced to work alone (many teachers still view collaboration as cheating).

For all the good intentions and diligent work of computer science educators, students find introductory computer science courses very frustrating—so frustrating that typically one quarter of the students drop out of the classes and many others perform poorly. A recent informal e-mail survey indicated that the percentage of students doing poorly in, failing, or withdrawing from introductory classes is often as high as 50 percent nationally. People who have programmed for a while have learned to live through extensive debugging sessions. A few too many debugging sessions, especially long ones, and beginning students might decide this is not the right career path for them. One anticipated outcome of the research is to improve the retention of computer science students because they are less frustrated and more effective when working with a partner.

In particular, this study looks at the retention of the decreasing population of female and minority computer science students. We are encouraged by research that African-American success rates can be dramatically improved in science courses by shifting the learning paradigm from individual study to a paradigm that capitalizes on group processes, such as student work groups and student-student tutoring (Nelson 1996). The pair-learning approach is, of course, such a group process.

Initial unpublished results at North Carolina State and published results from UC, Santa Cruz (McDowell et al. 2002), indicate that students do appear to learn better when working in pairs. At North Carolina State, the paired students averaged 5 points higher on exams (without their partners, of course) than did the solo programmers. UC, Santa Cruz, pair programmers had an average score of 86 percent on programming projects while solo programmers averaged 67 percent. The pairing students at UC, Santa Cruz, had a retention rate of 92 percent while the solo students had a retention rate of 76 percent. We currently feel that pair programming is an effective pedagogical tool for teaching introductory students.

References

Bishop, G. (2000). *The Office of Real Soon Now*, http://www.cs.unc.edu/~gb/office.htm.

Bishop, G. and Welch, G. (2000). "Working in the Office of 'Real Soon Now,'" *IEEE Computer Graphics and Applications,* July/August 2000, pp. 76–78.

Coplien, J. O. (2002). *Developing in Pairs*, http://i44pc48.info.uni-karlsruhe.de/cgi-bin/OrgPatterns?DevelopingInPairs.

Fagan, M. E. (1976). "Advances in Software Inspections to Reduce Errors in Program Development," *IBM Systems Journal*, vol. 15, pp. 182–211.

Fish, R. S., Kraut, R. E., and Chalfonte, B. L. (1990). *The VideoWindow System in Informal Communications*, presented at Proc. of CSCW '90, Los Angeles.

Kircher, M., Jain, P., Corsaro, A., and Levine, D. (2001). *Distributed eXtreme Programming*, XP2001.

McDowell, C., Werner, L., Bullock, H., and Fernald, J. (2002). *The Effects of Pair Programming in an Introductory Programming Course*. SIGCSE Conference Computer Science Education 2002.

Nelson, E. (1996). "Student Diversity Requires Different Approaches to College Teaching, Even in Math and Science," *American Behavioral Scientist,* vol. 40, pp. 165–175.

Olson, G. M. and Olson, J. S. (2000). *Distance Matters*, presented at Human Computer Interaction.

Rascar, R., Welch, G., Cutts, M., Lake, A., Stesin, L., and Fuchs, H. (1998). *The Office of the Future: A Unified Approach to Image-Based Modeling and Spatially Immersive Displays*, SIGGRAPH.

Russell, G. W. (1991). "Experience with Inspection in Ultralarge-Scale Developments," *IEEE Software*, vol. 8, no. 1, pp. 25–31.

Weller, E. F. (1993). "Lessons from Three Years of Inspection Data," *IEEE Software*, vol. 10, no. 5, pp. 38–45.

chapter twenty-seven

Seven Habits of Effective Pair Programmers

To end the book, we summarize what we have found to be seven habits of effective pair programmers. Many of these techniques have been discussed throughout the book, but we consolidate our recommendations here. Chapter 3 talked about "synergistic behaviors" of pairs, but these are quite different. These seven habits should be deliberately practiced, and you should consciously remind yourself of them in order to be most effective.

Habit 1: Take Breaks

"Pair programming is exhausting but productive" (Wake 2002). Because pair programmers do keep each other continually focused and on-task, it can be very intense and mentally exhausting. Periodically taking a break is important for maintaining the stamina you need for another round of productive pair programming. During the break, it is best to disconnect from the task at hand and approach it with a freshness when you restart. During breaks, you can do all those things you've been putting off—check e-mail, return phone calls, surf the Web (for business related purposes, of course).

At a minimum, each hour stand up, stretch, and look at something more than three feet away!

Habit 2: Practice Humility

"Egoless programming," an idea expounded by Gerald Weinberg in *The Psychology of Computer Programming* (1998) a quarter of a century ago, is essential for effective pair programming. Excess ego can manifest itself in two ways, both damaging the collaborative relationship. First, having a "my way or the highway" attitude can prevent the programmer from considering others' ideas. Second, excess ego can cause a programmer to be defensive when receiving criticism or to view this criticism as mistrust. However, all must remember to put the team and progress above his or her own ego. Wins and losses are made by the team!

People who are considered "experts" on their teams might be concerned about pairing because they might have to reveal to their partner that there's something they don't know (which might make them feel a bit lower on the pedestal). However, none of us, no matter how skilled, is infallible or above the input of another. John von Neumann, the great mathematician and creator of the von Neumann computer architecture, recognized his own inadequacies and continually asked others to review his work.

> And indeed, there can be no doubt of von Neumann's genius. His very ability to realize his human limitation put him head and shoulders above the average programmer today . . . Average people can be trained to accept their humanity—their inability to function like a machine— and to value it and work with others so as to keep it under the kind of control needed if programming is to be successful. (Weindberg 1998)

Weinberg (1998) also shares a true scenario about a programmer seeking review of the code he produced. On this particular "bad programming" day, this individual egolessly laughed because his reviewer found seventeen bugs in thirteen statements. However, after these defects were fixed, this code performed flawlessly during test and in production. Think how much worse the programmer's life would have been if he'd been too proud to accept the input of others or had viewed this input as an indication of his inadequacies. One of pair programming's biggest benefits is the continuous, objective review of design and coding. "The human eye has an almost infinite capacity for not seeing what it does not want to see . . . Programmers, if left to their own devices, will ignore the most glaring errors in their output—errors that anyone else can see in an instant" (Weinberg 1998). Learn to laugh at yourself!

Everyone should be ready to switch between mentor and student minute by minute. Take the opportunities to learn and teach as they arise.

Habit 3: Be Confident/Be Receptive

It can be very difficult to work with people who have great insecurity or anxiety about their programming skills. They tend to have an "If I work with you, you might find out I've never coded with exceptions" defensiveness about them. Programmers with such insecurity should view pair programming as a means to improve their skill by constantly watching and obtaining feedback from another. It will also make you feel more confident when you realize first-hand that no one knows everything, and many don't know as much as you thought they did.

A fear of appearing stupid also decreases the number of bold proposals and ideas suggested. Conversely, programmers who are comfortable working with their partners will offer intriguing suggestions and interesting strategies with the knowledge that their counterparts feel comfortable doing the same. (Dick and Zarnett 2002, Cockburn and Williams 2001)

There should be no competition between the partners; both must work for a singular purpose, as if the artifact was produced by a single good mind. Blame for problems or defects should never be placed on either partner. The pair needs to trust each other's judgment and each other's loyalty to the team.

Habit 4: Communicate

Communication between the pair is essential. Again we recommend that not more than a minute pass without some form of communication between the pair. One pair programmer says, "When I pair, 15 seconds without talking is a very long time; 30 seconds is an eternity. It's not hard (and is very important) to learn to type while talking; good pairs talk a lot." This might seem unachievable for programmers who are often thought of as extreme introverts. Alistair Cockburn and Pete McBreen share their perspectives:

> Programmers are typically stereotyped as noncommunicative individuals who like to sit in darkened rooms alone with their computer screens. It is not a true stereotype, though. Programmers just like to communicate about things they like to communicate about, usually the programs they are involved in. Programmers enjoy trading notes about XML-RPC or the difficulties in mapping object-ori-

ented designs to relational databases. They just don't like to join in the chitchat about things they consider irrelevant. (Cockburn 2002)

Developers are not expected to turn into extroverts. They are expected to do what they excel at—namely, to show their colleagues what they are working on; to look at what their colleagues are doing to see what they can learn; to spot as many loopholes, flaws, and mistakes as possible . . . Not even the most introverted geeks will find this requirement hard in a small team of people they know and trust. (McBreen 2002)

In the pairing context, Ward Cunningham, one of the founders of XP, recommends the driver practice a *reflective articulation* (Chi et al. 1989) technique and continually vocalize "self-explanations." As the driver, vocalize what you are doing as you are doing it. Be sure to speak loudly and clearly enough so that your partner can hear and understand you. For example, "We need to create a temporary variable here to accumulate the values as we iterate" or "Now we'll call the SortedByLastName method that will return all the records in the database sorted by last name."

Reflective articulation has been studied a great deal by sociology and education scholars (Narayanan et al. 1995). In the pair programming context, this reflective articulation has several benefits. First, we can identify flaws in our own logic simply by explaining it to someone else. Second, it keeps the navigator engaged because there is constant communication with him or her. The navigator can follow what is going on much more and can help much more if he or she understands what you are trying to do and where you are going.

Habit 5: Listen

If I were to summarize in one sentence the single most important principle I have learned in the field of interpersonal relations, it would be this: Seek first to understand, then to be understood. (Covey 1989)

Really listen to what your partner has to say before responding. Don't assume you know what he or she is talking about or that he or she understands what you are trying to do. Listen to the details of what he or she is saying. Don't assume he or she is trying to insult you or to criticize your ideas. Until proven wrong, assume your partner is just trying to get the job done.

Believe that through listening to your partner, your joint knowledge can be synergized. Human beings can remember and learn only a bounded amount. Therefore humans must consult with others to increase this bounded amount. When two are working together, each has his or her own set of knowledge and skills. A large subset of this knowledge and these skills will be common between the two, allowing them to interact effectively. However, the unique skills of each individual will allow the pair to engage in interactions that pool their resources to accomplish their tasks. "Collaborative people are those who identify a possibility and recognize that their own view, perspective, or talent is not enough to make it a reality. Collaborative people see others not as creatures who force them to compromise, but colleagues who can help them amplify their talents and skills" (Hargrove 1998).

Habit 6: Be a Team Player

The most important thing to remember about being a navigator is that your partner's work is your work. It is joint work that you are 100 percent responsible for. It is not acceptable to say or think things such as, "You made an error in your design" or "That defect was from your part." Say instead, "We screwed up the design" or, better yet, "We just got through our test with no defects!" Both partners own everything.

If you are a navigator, you should feel confident that you can take over as driver at any moment. If you don't feel this way, ask to be the driver so you will be forced to understand what is going on.

Once you believe this, it will be easier to remain active and engaged. You wouldn't want the driver to screw up your work while you're daydreaming, would you? You need constantly to be alert and questioning. If you don't understand what's going on, ask! If you can think of a better way, suggest it!

Habit 7: Hone the Balance between Compromise and Standing Firm

Developers who are too egotistical may lack the ability to compromise and may become argumentative when paired. The primary purpose of pairing is to work toward the best design possible, regardless of from where or from whom the design originated. Good development pairs can discuss suggestions without bias concerning their origin, and they can deliberate solely on the merits of the suggestions. (Dick and Zarnett 2002) It is very frustrating to work with a partner who flat out refuses to accept any suggestions. Before long, the navigator will assume his or her input will just be refuted and will give up making suggestions.

Conversely, people who always agree with their partners lest they create tension also minimize the benefits of collaborative work. For favorable idea exchange, there should be some healthy disagreement/debate.

Finding the balance between standing firm and compromising is a tricky one. If you really believe that you have a better way but your partner does not agree, use some of the techniques discussed in Chapter 11—separate and prototype, and so on. As you each pursue your idea further, the better idea should be more evident. Don't be afraid or unwilling to give up to the better idea. The goal is for the pair to produce the best possible.

Choose your battles wisely. We learn this lesson raising children. As much as you really want that kid to wear blue socks, does it really matter if he or she insists on wearing white socks? If your partner really wants a do-while loop but you think it would be better as a for loop, think about whether it really makes a difference in this case before being insistent or argumentative.

Finale

Practice these tried-and-true habits, and you should become a more effective partner. Old habits can be hard to break. Most of us have programmed for (many) years before venturing into pairing. Keep in mind that individuals out for themselves may not be maximizing the team performance. Let go of old habits for the benefit of your team, and have more fun in the process. You've got someone to bounce your good ideas off and someone who'll be bouncing good ideas off you. You've got someone whose work you can help improve and someone who'll help you when you do something imperfect. If software development is sometimes scary, you've got someone to help drive out the fear. If software development is a game, then you've got someone to play with; that might seem scary, but it's a lot more fun!

References

Chi, M. T. H., Bassok, M., Lewis, M. W., Reimann, P., and Glaser, R. (1989). "Self-Explanations: How Students Study and Use Examples in Learning to Solve Problems, *Cognitive Science,* Vol. 13, pp. 145–182.

Cockburn, A. and Williams, L. (2003). "The Costs and Benefits of Pair Programming," in *Extreme Programming Perspectives*, Addison-Wesley, in press.

Covey, S. R. (1989). *The Seven Habits of Highly Effective People*, Simon & Schuster.

Dick, A. J. and Zarnett, B. (2002). "Paired Programming and Personality Traits," submitted to XP2002.

Hargrove, R. (1998). *Mastering the Art of Creative Collaboration,* McGraw-Hill.

McBreen, P. (2002). *Software Craftsmanship: The New Imperative,* Addison-Wesley.

Narayanan, N. H., Hmelo, C. E., Petrushin, V., Newstetter, W. C., Guzdial, M., and Kolodner, J. L. (1995), "Computational Support for Collaborative Learning Through Generative Problem Solving," Proceedings of Computer Supported Collaborative Learning.

Wake, W. C. (2002). *Extreme Programming Explored,* Addison-Wesley.

Weinberg, G. M. (1998). *The Psychology of Computer Programming Silver, Anniversary Edition*. Dorset House Publishing.

Pair Programming Tutorial

As we've said before, people are often resistant to trying pair programming but then are quite enthusiastic once they've actually tried it. A good way to get people—programmers and managers alike—indoctrinated into the benefits of pair programming is to take them through a half-day pair programming exercise. In Appendix A, we outline such an exercise. Note that this exercise requires no programming experience, so it should be appropriate to everyone—programmers, managers, QA, and so on.

This exercise has been run as a tutorial at several conferences, including OOPSLA and NASA's Software Engineering Workshop. PowerPoint slides with notes for this exercise can be found at:

http://www4.ncsu.edu/~lawilli3/PP/tutorial.ppt.

Outline of the Exercise

Here is an overview of a three-hour workshop. In this chapter, we will describe the activities of each of the parts.

Content Outline for Half-Day Exercise (3 Hours)

Welcome and Exercise Objectives (5 minutes)
Activity I: Pair Understanding (15 minutes)
Research Results in Pair Programming Presentation (40 minutes)
Activity II: Individual Design (15 minutes)
Break (20 minutes)
Adoption of Pair Programming Presentation (20 minutes)
Activity III: Individuals Working on a Team (20 minutes)
Pair Programming Implementation Items Presentation (20 minutes)

Activity IV: Pairs Rotating Around a Team (20 minutes)
Summary and Conclusion (5 minutes)

Welcome and Exercise Objectives (5 Minutes)

Welcome the participants. Depending on how well participants know each other, you can have them introduce themselves and explain what they hope to gain by participating in the exercise. Feel free to insert any warm-up exercise of your choice. (Only five minutes of the three hours have been allocated to this activity. Warm-up exercises can be great ice breakers, but you may need to consider time contraints.)

Next, explain the learning objectives of the exercise:

1. Participants will experience the difference between working alone and working in pairs.

2. Participants will learn about pair programming research results.

3. Participants will learn tips for transitioning to pair programming.

Activity I: Pair Understanding (15 Minutes)

A wonderful benefit of working with a partner is that he or she can fill in gaps on knowledge. Where each person in the pair might only know or understand 75 percent of what is required, together they can strive for 100 percent understanding. To gain this full understanding, each person asks questions and uses the other as a sounding board. Ultimately, the pair reaches a point where they feel quite confident and comfortable moving forward to make progress; they have gained pair understanding.

The first activity in the exercise is intended to simulate the gaining of pair understanding. The exercise begins with a description of something that the participants are not familiar with. The description should be fairly logical but not overly clear. After hearing the description, participants should intentionally have the feeling, "I think I understand what you are saying, but I'm not exactly sure." For example, following is a description of Organizational Patterns (Coplien 1995) that can be used for an audience not overly familiar with the technique of using such patterns:

We'll spend today talking about pair programming. Pair programming is not actually such a new concept. There have definitely been people doing pair programming for quite a long time. In fact, Jim Coplien identified pair programming as an organizational pattern back in the middle of the 1990s. He called the pattern "Developing in Pairs." How many of you are familiar with organizational patterns (hopefully, not the majority of the audience)? Perhaps it's appropriate if we start by discussing organizational patterns.

First, we need to start by explaining what a pattern is. In computer science, many different kinds of patterns have emerged. For example, Martin Fowler has a book on analysis patterns (1997) and the Gang of Four has a book on design patterns (Gamma et al. 1995). All these patterns were inspired by the work of a building architect, Christopher Alexander (Alexander et al. 1977). Alexander describes a pattern: "Each pattern describes a problem which occurs over and over again in our environment and then describes the core of the solution to that problem, in such a way that you can use this solution a million times over, without ever doing it the same way twice."

Considering Alexander's description of patterns, organizational patterns are patterns applied to organizations, problems that occur in organizations and a general solution to that problem. For example, let's discuss the "Developing in Pairs" organizational pattern. A pattern describes a problem, which in this case is "People are scared to solve problems alone." And the pattern describes the core of the solution to that problem, which is pair programming.

Just to make sure that we all understand what patterns are, let's see if you can name some patterns that exist in your own organizations. . . . Remember, the pattern has a problem and a general solution. Think for a minute, and then share some of the patterns you have in your own organization.

At this point, the exercise facilitator gives the participants a minute or so to think of organizational patterns and then asks for people voluntarily to share their organizational patterns with the group. The desired result is that the group will provide very little input. If it appears there is an organizational pattern expert in the group, let him or her share no more than two patterns before saying, "I'd like to hear from someone else." It is likely that people will not share because the description of organizational patterns was not overly clear. It could have been made clearer with the addition of some examples.

Next the facilitator can say, "In order to make organizational patterns more clear, let's work in pairs. Between the two of you, try to come up with two or three patterns you have in your organization. Remember once gain that a pattern has a problem and a general solution as the 'Developing in Pairs' pattern showed us." Then give the pairs no more than five minutes to come up with some patterns. Ask again for pairs to share their organizational patterns voluntarily. The desired result is that pairs are now overflowing with organizational patterns.

Individually, each person might not have fully understood organizational patterns. Once each individual had someone to work with, the pair did two things. First, they clarified each other's understanding of organizational patterns. They asked each other questions until they both had a good comprehension of what the organizational patterns are. Second, each person was a sounding board for the other. One could say, "I think 'stand-up meetings' are a pattern. The problem is lack of daily communication; the solution is a stand-up meeting. Do you think that is a pattern?" If the partner says "Yes, that's definitely a pattern. That's a great pattern." Once receiving that validation, the participant will then confidently share this with the entire group.

The facilitator should point out the lesson of the exercise: Pairs help each other gain full understanding and help each other gain confidence for moving forward.

Research Results in Pair Programming (40 minutes)

The first section of the PowerPoint slides are reviewed. Notes explaining each slide are included with the presentation. The 40 minutes allow time for questions and group discussion. The slides include

- A Definition of Pair Programming

- A Historical Perspective of Pair Programming

- Research Results

- Synergistic Behaviors of Pair Programmers

Activity II: Individual Design (15 minutes)

For the next activity, the group is shown a problem statement for a transportation device. The device needs to be able to

- Transport people faster than they can move by walking, but it must go less than 10 mph.

- Stop on demand.

- Carry at least one person.

- Restrain passengers so they don't fall out.

- Look nice.

Participants are asked to spend approximately five minutes designing their device. At the end of this time, the participants are placed into groups of four. They share their design with their group. Specifically, each group should discuss the aspects that are common and unique among each design. Approximately five minutes should be allotted for this sharing.

Then all exercise participants discuss the exercise for five minutes. The discussion should focus on the similarities and differences among the individual designs.

The facilitator should point out the lesson of the exercise: When engineers work individually on a design, there will be some similarities among the designs. However, each engineer will typically incorporate a larger number of unique features.

Break (20 minutes)

Adoption of Pair Programming Presentation (20 minutes)

The PowerPoint slides from the second section are reviewed. Notes explaining each slide are included with the presentation. The allotted 20 minutes allows time for questions and group discussion. The slides include

- Managerial Resistance

- How to Gain Acceptance from Peers

- Transitioning by Choice

Activity III: Individuals Working on a Team (15 minutes)

Participants stay with the group of four they worked with in Activity II. For the next activity, the group is shown another, slightly different, problem statement for a transportation device. The device needs to be able to

- Transport people faster than 10 mph but slower than 100 mph.

- Stop on demand.

- Carry at least one person.

- Restrain passengers so they don't fall out.

- Look nice.

Each participant is given the assignment of completing one aspect of the transportation device design. The four roles are: Appearance, Propelling System, Braking System, Restraint System. Each participant must complete his or her assignment without collaborating with the team. Approximately two minutes are given for this activity. At this time, each participant is asked to draw the entire transportation device, again without collaborating with team members (approximately two minutes). Last, the team members must integrate their design into one transportation device. The integrated device must take the appearance from the one participant in charge of appearance, the braking system from the participant who designed that, and so on. This should take approximately five minutes. The remaining six minutes are spent on a discussion of how far each person's individual view of the system was from the integrated device. It is fun to make this point by having selected participant teams draw their own view and their integrated view on transparency slides. Then these teams can show the entire workshop each individual view versus their integrated device. Additionally, it is likely that the integrated device will not have components that do not logically fit together.

The facilitator should point out the lessons of the exercise: When engineers work individually on a design, the components may not fit together when integrated. Additionally, individuals do not have a good feel for the overall design of the project.

Pair Programming Implementation Items Presentation (20 minutes)

The Power Point slides are from the third section of reviewed. Notes explaining each slide are included with the presentation. The 20 minutes allow time for questions and group discussion. The slides include

- Good/Bad Pairs

- Pair Rotation

- Workspace Layout

- Other Items

Activity IV: Pairs Rotating Around a Team (20 minutes)

Participants stay with the group of four they worked with in Activity III. For the next activity, the group is shown another, slightly different, problem statement for a transportation device. The device needs to be able to

- Transport people faster than 100 mph.

- Stop on demand.

- Carry at least one person.

- Restrain passengers, so they don't fall out.

- Look nice.

Each participant is assigned a specific role in the design of the device. The four roles are Appearance, Propelling System, Braking System, Restraint System. Each participant is given ultimate authority of that aspect of the device in the upcoming collaborative effort. Each participant must complete his or her assignment without collaborating with the team. A rotation of pairs then takes place.

1. Each participant is assigned a partner to work with. Together the pair works on the two things they were assigned for two minutes.

2. Partners rotate so that each person is paired with a team member he or she did not yet work with. Together the pair work on the two things they were assigned for two minutes.

3. Partners rotate again so that each person is paired with the last team member he or she did not work with. Together the pair works on the two things they were assigned for two minutes.

At this time, each participant is asked to draw the entire transportation device—again without collaborating with team members (approximately two minutes). Last, the team members must integrate their design into one transportation device. The integrated device must take the appearance from the one participant in charge of appearance, the braking system from the participant who designed that, and so on. This should take approximately three minutes. The remaining four minutes are spent on a discussion of how far people's individual view of the system was from the integrated device. Again, it is fun to make this point by having selected participant teams draw their own view and their integrated view on transparency slides. Then these teams can show the entire workshop each individual view versus their integrated device. Hopefully, the individuals have a better view of the overall device than they did in the previous exercise.

The facilitator should point out the lessons of the exercise: Pairs that rotate around a group have a better understanding of the entire project. Additionally, the components that are designed by pairs that rotate around the group are more likely to fit together into a cohesive system.

Summary and Conclusion (5 minutes)

At the end of the session, the facilitator should point out again the lessons learned from the exercise. A learning objective of the session was for people to experience pair programming first-hand. This was done through the activities. Added objectives of the activities were to show that pair programming can be used to spread system knowledge better around a group and to aid in individual components formulating one cohesive system when integrated. Additionally, participants learned about research results of pair programming, and they acquired hints and tips about transitioning to pair programming.

After reviewing the objectives of the exercise, the facilitator should ask for participant feedback and should allow an open discussion on implementing pair programming in the organization. This kind of discussion would certainly take more than five minutes, but it should be very valuable.

References

Alexander, C., Ishikawa, S., Silverstein, M., Jacobson, M., Fiksdale, I. and Angel, S. (1977). *A Pattern Language.* Oxford University Press.

Coplien, J. O. (1995). "A Development Process Generative Pattern Language," in *Pattern Languages of Program Design*, James O. Coplien and Douglas C. Schmidt, eds., Addison-Wesley, pp. 183–237.

Fowler, M. (1997). *Analysis Patterns: Reusable Object Models*, Addison-Wesley.

Gamma, E., Helm, R., Johnson, R., Vlissides, J. (1995). *Design Patterns: Elements of Reusable Object-Oriented Software*, Addison-Wesley.

An Economic Analysis of Pair Programming

by Hakan Erdogmus and Laurie Williams

In this appendix, we present a detailed economic analysis of pair programming based on the empirical study conducted at the University of Utah, as discussed in Chapter 4. (You should probably read Chapter 4 before reading this appendix because we won't go back over the details of the experiment.) In Chapter 4, we indicated that pairs produce higher-quality code but that it might take 15 percent longer to produce this higher-quality code. Once code is written, it then goes on to testing and ultimately to the customer. When you consider the savings of putting higher-quality code into test and into the hands of the customer, our economic analysis shows that this initial 15 percent cost is more than made up for. We write this appendix for the reader who would like to know more about how we can claim the overall life-cycle affordability of pair programming.

Introduction

The economic feasibility of pair programming is a key issue. Many people instinctively reject pair programming because they think that code development costs will double. If it is more expensive, managers simply will not permit it. Naturally, the goal of a software firm is to be as profitable as possible while providing customers with the best, high-quality products quickly and cheaply. Organizations decide whether to adopt process improvements based on the business value of their outcome.

First we compute and analyze a basic comparison of the processes. This basic comparison indicates that pairs perform better with regard to efficiency and overall productivity. We further this basic comparison by incorporating additional factors into a more complex Net Present Value (NPV) analysis. This economic comparison indicates that pair programming should be considered as an economical alternative over solo programming. NPV considers the time value of money: the premise that a dollar today is worth more than a dollar in the future. Economic models based on NPV have previously been suggested to evaluate the return on software quality and infrastructure initiative (Boehm 1981; Erdogmus 1999; Erdogmus and Vendergraaf 1999; Favaro et al. 1998; Levy 1987).

Factors of the Basic Comparison Model

Sound research design guides us to have only one experimental variable, the variable under study. Programmers create software using a variety of software development practices. We ensured that all programmers in the study used all the same practices (for design, testing, etc.) except for the experimental variable, the *work unit*: solo programmer versus pair of programmers working in tandem. In our analysis, we refer to the work unit as follows:

- N: *size of the work unit* (persons). The number of developers in a work unit. N equals 1 for a solo programmer (hereby, a *soloist*), and 2 for a pair of programmers (hereby, a *pair*).

The values of the several model variables we use are determined based on past research studies and statistics reported in the literature. The chosen values are primarily for illustration purposes. The actual values could be different, and they would most likely be both project- and skill-dependent. However, we believe the general conclusions we make are still sound with reasonable variability of these values.

- π. *new-code productivity* (LOC/person-hour). The average per-person hourly output (LOC) of new code for the work unit.

    According to a study by Hayes and Over (1997), the average productivity rate of 196 developers who took PSP training was 25 LOC/hour. This figure will be the chosen value of π for $N = 1$ (soloist).

Anectodal evidence (Wiki 1999; Auer and Miller 2001) suggests that pairing does not take any additional time over solo programming. However, the University of Utah experiment indicated that pairs might take 15 percent more time than solo programmers. In our analysis, we are conservative and assume that the observed 15 percent difference is real (despite the fact that, statistically speaking, this difference was insignificant). With this assumption, in a single person-hour, each developer of a pair produces an average of $25/(1.15) = 22$ LOC. Thus for $N = 1$ we use $\pi = 25$ LOC/person-hour and for $N = 2$, π is taken to be a conservative 22 LOC/person-hour.

■ β. *defect rate* (defects/LOC). The average number of defects per unit of output (LOC) associated with the work unit.

According to Jones (1997), code produced in the United States has an average of 39 raw defects per KLOC. This statistic is based on data collected from such companies as AT&T, Hewlett-Packard, IBM, Microsoft, Motorola, and Raytheon, with formal defect tracking and measurement capabilities. According to the same reference, on average, 85 percent of all raw defects are removed via the development process, and 15 percent escape to the client.

Together the two pieces of statistics suggest an average defect rate of $(39)(0.15) = 6$ defects/KLOC. This figure represents defects that escape to the customer. The number is consistent, although on the low side, with data from the Pentagon and the Software Engineering Institute, which indicates that typical software applications contain five to fifteen defects per KLOC (Gross et al. 1999). We adopt the average six defects/KLOC (or .006 defects/LOC) as the value of β for $N = 1$ (soloist).

As discussed in Chapter 4, the code written by the pairs in the experiment passed an average of 90 percent of the specified acceptance tests compared with code written by soloists, which passed on average only 75 percent of the same test suite. This result suggests that, after acceptance tests, pairs have only 40 percent of the defects that solo programmers have. If we assume that this ratio is retained in defects that escape to the customer, we can adopt as the value of β for $N = 2$ (pair) is $(6)(0.4) = 2.4$ defects/KLOC.

- ρ. *rework speed* (defects/person-hour). The speed at which defects are fixed by the work unit following the deployment of a piece of code.

A study of a set of industrial software projects from a large telecommunications company (Russel 1991) showed that each defect found by a customer required an average of 4.5 person-days, or 33 person-hours, of subsequent maintenance effort or rework (based on a 7.5-hour workday). This statistic is consistent with data reported by Humphrey (1995). Based on this observation, the rework speed ρ for $N = 1$ (soloist) is taken to be $1/33 = 0.03$ defects/person-hour.

No data is available regarding the effect of pair development on rework activities. We will assume pairs will perform rework with the same 15 percent cost relative to soloists as was found in the experiment. Under this assumption, the estimated rework speed ρ for $N = 2$ will be $0.03/1.15 = 0.026$ defects/person-hour.

The Basic Comparison Model

In the basic comparison model, we compare two metrics, ε (*efficiency*) and π_0 (*overall productivity*).

Efficiency

Efficiency is defined as the percentage effort spent on developing new code relative to the total life-cycle effort (which includes the effort expended on rework).

Given a productivity rate of π, the effort required in person-hours to deploy ω lines of code of output is given by

$$E_{pre} := \frac{\omega}{\pi}$$

This quantity specifies the *initial development* (or *predeployment*) *effort* and is followed by *rework* (or *postdeployment*) *effort* once the code has been delivered to the client.

Rework effort, E_{post}, is the maintenance effort expended due to runaway defects after a piece of new code has been deployed.

$$E_{post}: = \frac{\omega\beta}{\rho}$$

Here $\omega\beta$ is the number of defects, and ρ is the speed of rework. Effort is always adjusted to the work unit by multiplying it by the work unit size N.

Total effort, E_{tot}, is the sum of the initial development and rework efforts:

$$E_{tot}: = \frac{\omega(\rho + \beta\pi)}{\pi\rho}$$

Efficiency, ε, is then the ratio of the initial development effort E_{pre} to the total effort E_{tot}. It is given by:

$$\varepsilon: = \frac{\rho}{\rho + \beta\pi}$$

The percentage effort spent on rework then equals $1 - \varepsilon$, or:

$$\frac{\beta\pi}{\rho + \beta\pi}$$

Overall Productivity

Overall productivity, π_0, is the average hourly output of defect-free code per programmer hour (assuming that the code is defect free after rework). It equals the total output ω in LOC divided by the total effort E_{tot} in person-hours. This measure shows just how much the "realized productivity" can be dominated by the extensive cost of rework late in the life cycle. Expressed in terms of efficiency and new-code productivity, overall productivity is given by

$$\pi_0 = \pi\varepsilon$$

Results

Table B-1 compares a soloist to a pair with respect to the efficiency, new-code productivity, and overall productivity metrics. In each row, the cell in bold type indicates the more favorable alternative with respect to the corresponding metric. Pairs fair considerably better in efficiency and overall productivity, indicating that initial investments in quality during pair programming pays for itself over the product life cycle.

Table B-1 Comparison of a soloist to a pair

	Soloist	Pair
Efficiency (ε) (decimal percent)	.17	**.34**
New-code productivity (π) (LOC/person-hour)	**25**	22
Overall productivity (π_0) (LOC/person-hour)	4.3	**7.4**

Factors of the Economic Comparison Model

The second comparison model is more complex than the basic comparison model and considers additional important factors that determine economic feasibility.

A software project incurs costs as it accumulates labor hours and realizes value as it delivers functionality. A project is economically feasible when the total value it creates exceeds the total cost it incurs. We assume that the net value generated depends on (1) the project's labor cost, (2) the time value of money/present value, and (3) the value that the project earns proportionate with the output it produces. The following sections discuss the factors and the underlying parameters that will be used in the advanced analysis.

Labor Cost

Programmer labor (C) is often the most important cost driver in a software development project. We will assume that initial development and rework are performed by the same work unit, resulting in the same constant value for both variables. Because C is assumed to be invariant, we will later be able to eliminate it using a ratio metric.

Time Value of Money and Present Value

When costs and benefits of a project are spread over time, the time at which the costs are incurred and the benefits are realized must be taken into account. A cash flow expected to occur in the future is worth less in today's dollars than a cash flow that occurs now. As the time horizon widens, the difference between the value of a dollar today and the value of a dollar in the future also widens. Time value of money captures the spread between these two values. *Discounting* is the process of downward adjusting a future cash flow to express it in today's value using a compound interest rate, called the *discount rate*. The discounted value of the cash flow is referred to as the *present value* (PV).

In economic terms, cost and benefits of a project are represented as negative and positive cash flows, respectively, that occur at specific points in time. The fundamental implication of time value of money is that a project should earn as fast as possible and spend as slow as possible to generate maximum economic benefit.

Earned Value

Earned value (*EV*) expresses the output produced by a work unit using a linear relationship between development effort and value. Each unit of new code produced earns a fixed amount of value. We assume that rework effort does earn value. Only projects that are 100 percent efficient earn extra value for each labor hour, creating a disincentive to produce defective code and, conversely, an incentive to produce quality code.

Let *unit value*, V, refer to the average value earned by one unit of output produced. In our case, V is the average value of a single line of new code. Then, earned value corresponding to an output of ω lines of code is given by

$$EV: = V\omega$$

Value Realization

Realized value is value that is realized by the client when a functional, defect-free product has been delivered to a customer. Earned value is not the same as realized value. For example, earned value may never be realized if a project fails to deliver a functional product to the client.

The Software Factory Model

For our economic analysis, we consider a value realization model called the *Software Factory*. New code is developed, deployed, and reworked in very small increments. Initial development of new code and rework of deployed code are intertwined in a never-ending cycle. Value is realized in very small increments as microchunks of new functionality are gradually delivered. Consequently, earned and realized value are essentially the same. The Software Factory model is illustrated in Figure B-1. The ticks represent microdeployment points where small chunks of new code are delivered incrementally. In the perfect (idealized) version of the Software Factory model, the distance between two deployment points approaches zero, resulting in a truly continuous process. Emerging agile software development methodologies (Fowler 2000) such as XP (Beck et al. 2001) and SCRUM (Rising 2000) support frequent delivery of working code to customers. Agile methodologies are best treated under the Software Factory.

Defect Recovery Efficiency

Defect recovery efficiency involves two components: *latency* and *coverage*. Latency is the elapsed time between the deployment of a software artifact and the discovery of a fault by the client. Coverage is the number of defects reported or discovered in relation to the total number of defects (including those that have not been discovered). In practice, the discovery of defects by the client can be neither instantaneous nor complete. For example, Jones (1997) states that in large industrial projects, more than half of the defects in customer code have a latency of one year, while total coverage four years after deployment hovers around 97 percent.

In emerging, agile processes, continual testing and frequent client feedback are believed to lead to a defect recovery with low latency and high cov-

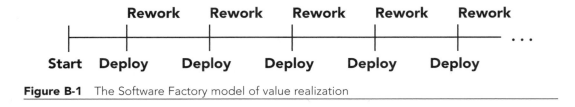

Figure B-1 The Software Factory model of value realization

erage. In our analysis, we assume a perfectly efficient defect recovery process—one with full coverage and zero latency. These idealized conditions are opposing in terms of their impact on net value generated. While increased coverage tends to decrease net value, increased latency tends to increase it. When time value of money is taken into account, these assumptions lead to a conservative overall bias with a mild tendency to underestimate net value. However, the level of underestimation may be different for different development processes.

The Economic Comparison Model

Net Present Value (*NPV*)

Capital investment decisions are often made based on the concept of Net Present Value (Ross 1996). Economic models based on *NPV* have previously been used to evaluate the return on software quality and infrastructure initiatives (Levy 1987; Boehm 1981; Erdogmus and Vandergraaf 1999; Favaro et al. 1998).

NPV is the difference between the present value of benefits and the present value of costs:

$$NPV = PV(benefits) - PV(costs),$$

where PV denotes present value.

A project is thought to have business value when its *Net Present Value*, *NPV*, is positive and to be unprofitable when its *NPV* is negative. Among a set of possible projects, the one with the highest *NPV* generates the most value and should be favored over the others.

For the Software Factory model, *NPV* reduces to

$$NPV^{\infty}: = IRV - TDC^{\infty}$$

Here *IRV* denotes *Incremental Realized Value* and *TDC* denotes *Total Discounted Cost*. Following is a discussion of each of these.

NPV is very sensitive to changes in *V*, the average value earned by one unit of output produced, measured in $/LOC. Figure B-2 shows how *NPV* varies

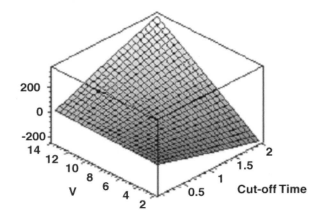

Figure B-2 *NPV* for a pair under the Software Factory model as a function of unit value *V* and cut-off time τ for a fixed annual discount rate of δ = 0.1. Output is plotted in KLOCs. Cut-off time, measured in years, represents the time horizon of the project. Labor cost is fixed at *C* = $50/hour.

as *V* and time horizon of the project increase for a pair under the Software Factory model, where the labor cost *C* is fixed at $50/hour. Note that the slope of the *NPV* curve changes drastically along the output axis as *V* varies.

Because of this sensitivity, our interest is not on *NPV* per se. We need a derived metric whose value can be used to rank two alternatives independent of a particular choice of unit value and of the constant labor cost *C*. *Breakeven Unit Value* meets the first need.

Breakeven Unit Value

Breakeven Unit Value (BUV) is the threshold value of *V* above which the *NPV* is positive. *BUV* is determined by solving the equation *NPV* = 0 for *V*. Recall that *V* is measured in $/LOC, based on the assumption that each unit of output produced increases the value earned by a constant amount.

A small *BUV* is better than a large *BUV*. As *BUV* increases, a project becomes less and less worthwhile because higher and higher margins are required to turn a profit. In the Software Factory model, *BUV* also makes the economic comparison independent of the particular choice of the discount rate.

BUV in the Software Factory

When both value realization and cost accumulation are continual and incremental, BUV's dependence on both output and discount rate is broken. However, BUV remains dependent on C, the hourly labor late.

For example, for a fixed labor cost of C = $50/person-hour, a soloist achieves a BUV of $12/LOC while a pair achieves a BUV of $7/LOC, indicating an advantage for the pair. These are the minimum marginal benefits required in the Software Factory for a project to break even.

Breakeven Unit Value Ratio (BUVR)

A comparison can be made between the return on investment offered by two different processes through an examination of the ratio of their BUVs.

Define BUV Ratio ($BUVR$) as the ratio of the BUV of a soloist to the BUV a pair.

$$BUVR = \frac{BUV_{solo}}{BUV_{pair}}$$

Values of $BUVR$ greater than unity indicate an advantage for pairs; values smaller than unity indicate an advantage for soloists. As this ratio increases, the advantage of the pair over the soloist also increases. The metric $BUVR$ makes the comparison between the two work units independent not only of V, but also of the hourly labor cost C.

BUV Ratio in the Software Factory

The BUV Ratio, $BUVR$, under the Software Factory model is given by

$$BUVR^{\infty} = \frac{\pi_{pair}\, \varepsilon_{pair}}{\pi_{solo}\, \varepsilon_{solo}}$$

Taking the ratio effectively eliminates the invariant C that appears in the BUV equation. The value of $BUVR$ is thus constant at 1.7, representing roughly a 40 percent advantage for the pairs over the soloist. Note that this advantage is independent of time value of money (discount rate), output produced, cut-off time (time horizon of the project), and labor cost. Effectively we obtain a metric that provides an all-around comparison.

Derivation of *BUV* Ratio

For those mathematically inclined readers, we now derive the *BUV* ratio. Otherwise, skip right to the summary at the end.

Marginal Value Earned

We need to consider *Marginal Value Earned* (*MVE*) in order to calculate *Incrementally Realized Value* (*IRV*), the first component in the *NPV* formula for the Software Factory. *MVE* is the average value earned per additional unit of elapsed time (measured in \$/year; elapsed time refers to compressed time). Given a completion or cut-off time of τ, *MVE* equals

$$MVE: = \frac{EV}{\tau} = \frac{V\omega}{\tau}$$

Representing output ω in terms of elapsed time eliminates the variable τ, allowing *MVE* to be expressed in terms of productivity π and efficiency ε. Let the constant h_y denote the total number of labor hours in a calendar year. Then *MVE* can be rewritten as

$$MVE: = V \, \pi \, \varepsilon \, h_y \, N$$

Incrementally Realized Value

Incrementally Realized Value (*IRV*) is the total value earned within a given time period. Value realized is discounted as earned. If τ is the time to project completion or the cut-off time, then *IRV* is given by

$$IRV: = \int_0^\tau MVE \, \mathbf{e}^{(-\delta\tau)} dt$$

Here δ denotes the continually compounded annual discount rate. (With continual compounding, the present value of a future cash flow X that occurs in t years is given by $Xe^{-\delta t}$.) Expressed in terms of efficiency ε and productivity π, IRV equals

$$IRV: = \frac{-V\,\pi\,\varepsilon\,h_y\,N(e^{(-\delta\tau)} - 1)}{\delta}$$

Marginal Cost

Marginal Cost (mC_∞) is the expected incremental cost of initial development and rework per additional unit of elapsed time. Because initial development and rework are intertwined in the Software Factory model, marginal cost can be written as

$$mC_\infty: = \frac{E\,\varepsilon\,C_{pre} + E\,(1 - \varepsilon)C_{post}}{\tau}$$

where E is the total effort. When pre- and postdeployment costs are equal (i.e., $C_{post} = C_{pre} = C$), marginal cost is simply

$$m\,C_\infty = h_y\,N\,C$$

Total Discounted Cost

In the Software Factory, labor costs are discounted as they are incurred to calculate the *Total Discounted Cost*, the second component of the *NPV* formula:

$$TDC_\infty: = \int_0^\tau mC_\infty e^{(-\delta\tau)}\,dt$$

After substituting the marginal cost with the corresponding term, the above definite integral reduces to

$$TDC_\infty: = -\frac{h_y\,N\,C\,(e^{(-\delta\tau)} - 1)}{\delta}$$

BUV in the Software Factory

BUV under the Software Factory model is obtained by solving the equation $NPV_\infty = IRV - TDC_\infty = 0$ for the unknown V. This yields

$$\mathrm{BUV}_\infty := \frac{C}{\pi \, \varepsilon}$$

The formula for the *BUV* Ratio immediately follows from this expression.

Summary

The results of our analyses demonstrate the potential of pair programming as an economically viable alternative to individual programming. Using the empirical results that demonstrated that pairs produce higher-quality code in 15 percent more time than individuals, we showed that pairs have a higher efficiency and overall productivity rate. Additionally, considering a more complex economic model, which considered Net Present Value, we demonstrated that pairs increase the business value of a project by significantly reducing the minimum marginal benefit required for a project to break even.

References

Auer, K. and Miller, R. (2002). *Extreme Programming: Playing to Win*, Addison-Wesley.

Basili, V., Shull, F., and Lanubile, F. (1999). "Building Knowledge Through Families of Experiments," *IEEE Transactions on Software Engineering*, vol. 25, pp. 456–473.

Beck, K. (2000). *Extreme Programming Explained: Embrace Change*, Addison-Wesley.

Beck, K. and Fowler, M. (2001). *Planning Extreme Programming*, Addison-Wesley.

Beck, K., Beedle, M., v. Bennekum, A., Cockburn, A., Cunningham, W., Fowler, M., Grenning, J., Highsmith, J., Hunt, A., Jeffries, R., Kern, J., Marick, B., Martin, R. C., Mellor, S., Schwaber, K., Sutherland, J., and Thomas, D. (2001). "The Agile Manifesto," http:// www.agileAlliance.org

Beck, K. and Cleal, D. (1999). "Optional Scope Contracts," http://www.xprogramming.com/ xpublications.htm.

Boehm, B. (1981). *Software Engineering Economics*, Prentice Hall.

Cockburn, A. and Williams, L. (2000). "The Costs and Benefits of Pair Programming," presented at eXtreme Programming and Flexible Processes in Software Engineering— XP2000, Cagliari, Sardinia, Italy.

Cockburn, A. and Williams, L. (2001). "The Costs and Benefits of Pair Programming," in *Extreme Programming Examined*, G. Succi and M. Marchesi, eds. Addison-Wesley, pp. 223–248.

Constantine, L. (1995). *Constantine on Peopleware*, Yourdon Press.

Coplien, J. O. (1995). "A Development Process Generative Pattern Language," in *Pattern Languages of Program Design*, James O. Coplien and Douglas C. Schmidt, eds., Addison-Wesley, pp. 183–237.

Erdogmus, H. (1999). "Comparative Evaluation of Software Development Strategies Based on Net Present Value," presented at International Conference on Software Engineering Workshop on Economics-Driven Software Engineering, CA.

Erdogmus, H. and Vandergraaf, J. (1999). "Quantitative Approaches for Assessing the Value of COTS-centric Development," presented at Sixth International Symposium on Software Metrics, Boca Raton, FL.

Favaro, J., Favaro, K., and Favaro, P. F. (1998). "Value-Based Software Reuse Investment," *Annals of Software Engineering*, vol. 5, pp. 5–52.

Fleming, Q. and Koppelman, J. (1998). "Earned Value Project Management: A Powerful Tool for Software Projects," *Crosstalk:* 19–23

Fowler, M. (2000). "Put Your Process on a Diet," in *Software Development*, vol. 8, 2000, pp. 32–36.

Gross, N., Stepanek, M., Port, O., and J. Carey (1999). "Software Hell," in *Business Week*, December, 1999, pp. 104–118.

Hayes, W. and Over, J. (1997). "The Personal Software Process: An Empirical Study of the Impact of PSP on Individual Engineers," Software Engineering Institute, Pittsburgh, PA CMU/SEI-97-TR-001, December 1997.

Jones, C. (1997). *Software Quality: Analysis and Guidelines for Success*, International Thomson Computer Press.

Humphrey, W. (1995). *A Discipline for Software Engineering*, Addison-Wesley.

Leby, L. (1987). *Taming the Tiger: Software Engineering and Software Economics*, Springer-Verlag.

Nosek, J. (1998). "The Case for Collaborative Programming," in *Communications of the ACM*, vol. March 1998, pp. 105–108.

Rising, L. and Janoff, N. (2000). "The Scrum Software Development Process for Small Teams," *IEEE Software*, vol. 17.

Ross, S. (1999). *Fundamentals of Corporate Finance*, Irwin/McGraw-Hill.

Russell, G. (1991). "Experience with Inspection in Ultralarge-Scale Developments," *IEEE Software*, vol. January 1991, pp. 25–31.

Succi, G. and Marchesi, M. (2001). *Extreme Programming Examined*. Addison-Wesley.

Wake, W. (2002). *Extreme Programming Explored*, Addison-Wesley.

Wiki (1999). "Programming in Pairs," in Portland Pattern Repository, accessed June 29, 1999, http://c2.com/cgi/wiki?ProgrammingInPairs.

Williams, L. (2000). "The Collaborative Software Process" Ph.D. Dissertation, Department of Computer Science, University of Utah.

Williams, L., Kessler, R., Cunningham, W., and Jeffries, R. (2000). "Strengthening the Case for Pair-Programming," in *IEEE Software*, vol. 17, pp. 19–25.

Williams, L. and Kessler, R. (2000). "All I Ever Needed to Know about Pair Programming I Learned in Kindergarten," in *Communications of the ACM*, vol. 43.

Pair Programming in the Classroom

The technique of pair programming has also been used in the undergraduate computer science classroom. In Appendix C, we'll explain the benefits we see to students and to educators. We'll also give some guidance to educators who would like to try pair programming in their classroom. We'd like to say, "Just have your students work in pairs—what's the big deal?" However, we realize that there are some problems and issues we want you to be prepared for. All in all, we can strongly encourage you to surmount the initial obstacles and adjust your classes to allow your students to work in pairs. It's good for you and good for them.

Benefits to Educators

Pair programming makes the instructor feel more positive about the class. Their students are happier, and the assignments are handed in on time and are of higher quality. The classes are calmer; the students are more satisfied and self-sufficient.

Another very positive effect for the teaching staff; there are fewer questions! The students no longer look to the teaching staff as their sole source of technical advice. The first time Laurie taught with pair programming, it was a Web programming class in 1999, when people didn't even know HTML. The students were very familiar with programming, but they were not familiar with the Active Server Pages (ASP) Web programming languages learned and used in the class. The majority of the students had used only WYSIWYG Web page editors prior to taking the class. During the eleven-week semester, the students learned advanced HTML, JavaScript, VBScript, Active Server Page Scripting, Microsoft Access/SQL, and some ActiveX commands. In many cases, the students would need to intertwine statements from all these languages into one program listing—some of the content running on the browser and some running on the NT server, adding to the overall complexity of the program. Upon course completion, the students were all writing Web scripts that had significant dynamic content that accessed and updated a Microsoft Access database—applications similar (although smaller) to what you would find on a typical ecommerce Web site. The remarkable thing was that students barely needed Laurie's help. During lab sessions, drivers were typing, and navigators were often flipping pages of books and class notes, guiding the drivers through the new techniques they had just learned and needed to apply. When one partner did not know or understand something, the other almost always did. Between the two of them, they could tackle anything.

The number of cheating cases is reduced because collaboration is legitimized. We believe that pair programming also cuts down on cheating because pair pressure causes the students to start working on projects earlier and to budget their time more wisely. Additionally, students have a peer to turn to for help and therefore do not feel as helpless.

Although it is probably obvious, we must mention that grading can be significantly reduced when two students submit one assignment. This does not mitigate the need to provide individual performance evaluation; however, it does reduce the load for those assignments done in pairs.

Benefits to Students

Pair programming reduces the frustration for many computer science students. As we all know, a small typo or a missing semicolon can cost hours of debugging time. Those of us who have programmed for years deal with this frustration. But students who are still choosing their career path must just give up on programming as a profession after a few bouts of six-hour debugging sessions. For all the good intentions and diligent work of computer science educators, students find introductory computer science courses very frustrating—so frustrating that typically one quarter of the students drop out of the classes and many others perform poorly. Having a continual reviewing of the navigator will reduce the need for these long, laborious debugging sessions. Rather than waiting minutes, hours, or even a day to get help from a teacher, pairs might be able to provide the answer immediately. Far less frustrating! We believe that data that is now being collected will ultimately show that pair programming reduces the drop-out rate of computer science graduates.

Students are much like the novice-novice pairs in Chapter 15. Students especially—female and minority students—often do a lot of negative self-talk. If they struggle with a program or a new programming construct, they often tell themselves that they must be the only ones who don't understand. They don't ask enough questions. If they were only smarter, they wouldn't need to ask questions. But, on the other hand, if they are working with a partner, one of two things can happen. First, their partner might explain something to them in a nonthreatening way (or they'll watch their partner do something and then understand it). Or, if they don't understand something and their partner doesn't understand something . . . well, then, it must be hard. (Negative self-talk is reduced.) They then have the conviction to ask for help—where solo students might suffer in silence, hour after hour.

As with industrial pairing, pairing in the classroom helps students get to know each other on a more personal basis. At most universities, class sizes are getting bigger. Students might feel like a just face in the crowd. However, if they are "forced" to work with a peer, they'll get to know that peer. Rotate the pairs, and they'll get to know many other peers. We're also hoping that research results will ultimately show that more women will be attracted to computer science if programming becomes more social and collaborative. Some researchers have distinct preferences for different kinds of environments (collaborative versus competitive, social versus individualistic) (Gilligan, 1982; Ruddick, 1989).

All in all, we've seen that students are happier and less frustrated. They have the camaraderie of another peer while they completed their assignments. Between the two in the pair, they could figure almost everything out. Students were more confident in their work. They felt good that they had a peer helping them to remove and prevent defects. They also felt good that they were better able to come up with more creative, efficient solutions when working with a partner.

Issues to Consider

Here are some hints and tips you and your students if you venture into the world of pair learning, that is, teaching your students programming through pair programming.

- Run as much of the Pair Programming Tutorial (Appendix A) as you can with your class. One would think that if you told students to work with a partner, they'd be very happy they didn't have to work alone. However, even students, especially more advanced undergraduates and graduates, need to be sold on the idea. Experiencing the benefits through the tutorial helps them with being sold.

- If at all possible, provide the students some class/lab time to work with their partner. During this time, the pair "bonds" by actually accomplishing something together and will generally plan their next meeting. During the required class/lab time, the teaching staff can ensure that the two are working together at one computer and that the roles of driver and observer are rotated.

  In our first semester of running paired labs, we were surprised to find the TAs were not very forceful with the students about pairing. If a student didn't want to pair, the TAs didn't make them pair. They never told the students it was time to rotate (driver and navigator). You will certainly need to coach your TAs, in fact, plan on it. Have them read this chapter! Also, we decided to purchase some funny looking kitchen timers and give one to each TA. It is standard operating procedure in the lab that "When the tomato timer dings, switch!"

- "Management by Walking Around," MBWA, that's what it's called in industry, anyway. Once students start working in pairs in the lab, the TA gets asked very few questions. TAs are generally students who have their own homework. The natural tendency is for them to sit at the TA computer and do their own homework if they are not asked questions by their class. If they ignore their class, the pairs could be behaving dysfunctionally—not respecting the tomato timer, one student doing all the work, one student slipping off to another computer to check his or her e-mail, and so on. We now explain to our TAs that they must walk around the lab and visit each pair several times during the lab period. The TA must fill out a little form with short observations of the working pair and hand this form in each week.

- To ensure the TAs are actually doing what they need to do, we suggest professors periodically drop by to see how things are going. There's more room for error with paired labs. Labs without pairs are event driven; the events are student questions. These events happen a lot and the TAs will generally fill their entire lab period by walking around and answering student questions. The TAs for paired labs must display more leadership and initiative: They must insist students work in pairs, rotate, and even out the work. They must be proactive about MBWA. Stopping in periodically will allow professors to make sure the right things are happening.

- We encourage you to change the makeup of the pairs periodically throughout the semester. There are several reasons to do this. First, it ensures no one is "stuck" with a bad partner for the entire semester. Doubtlessly, some students are more skilled than others. A more skilled student can tolerate a less skilled student if he or she doesn't feel responsible for the partner the whole semester. Pairs can also be more tolerant of their partner's poor hygiene or sloppy work habits if they are not "married" for the semester. Switching the pairs also aids in peer evaluation, which we'll talk about next. When two people work together, comments on contribution can end up being one person's word against another's. "He did nothing." "I did too! You did nothing." However, when you rotate partners throughout the semester, if every person a student pairs with says his or her partner didn't do anything, it's likely the partner really did do nothing. By the way, we also assign the pairs (using a Web-based program). We don't allow them to choose their own partners for the labs. We have a three-hour closed lab in which they complete their assignment. So we do not have to worry about the pairs having compatible schedules outside of class.

- Students need to have the motivation to contribute and not to ride on the coattails of their partner. Students need to be given a formal mechanism for reporting on the contributions of their partners and to provide a self-assessment of their own contribution. Whenever the students are about to switch to a new partner, we have them answer five short questions. They score their partner 0 (poor performance) to 20 (superior performance) on each of the following questions:

- Did the student read the lab and preparatory material before coming to the scheduled lab?

- Did the student do his or her fair share of the work?

- Did the student cooperatively follow the pair programming model (rotating roles of driver and navigator)?

- Did the student make contributions to the completion of the assignment?

- Did the student cooperate?

Based on their score on each of these five questions, students receive a peer evaluation score of 0 to 100 percent. We multiply the score they receive on their program by their peer evaluation score to get their lab score. For example, if they get 100 percent on their program and their peer evaluation score is a 50 percent (must not have been an effective partner), they get a 50 percent on their lab.

- The last few examples refer to classes that do have some form of lab. It is more challenging to integrate pair programming into a class in which there is no lab. Requiring students to work together without "forcing" them to start working together—because you have no lab setting for the forcing—can easily lead to failure. Students are very busy, and many do not want to take the extra effort to meet their partner in the lab. It's just easier to do the assignment in their dorm room, on their own computer, with the stereo blasting in their headphones. If you have no lab period, it would probably be best to make pair programming an optional arrangement for completing assignments, whereby students can choose between working alone or with a partner. We've also seen the suspicious results where students get 100 percent on projects where they paired and 30 percent on their exams. Hmmm, . . . something's fishy around here. Now our students have to earn the right to pair. In order to pair on an assignment, they must get above-average exam scores and higher than 90 percent on their peer evaluations.

We hope we didn't scare you with some of the issues we found or the suggestions we've made. We really do believe that pair learning is beneficial for the students and the instructor. There are some adjustments that need to be made. But, soon these adjustments will be normal procedures. It's worth it!

Resources

Bevan, J., Werner, L., and McDowell, C. (2002). *Guidelines for the Use of Pair Programming in a Freshman Programming Class,* Conference of Software Engineering Education and Training 2002.

Gilligan, C. (1982). *In a Different Voice: Psychological Theory and Women's Development,* Harvard University Press.

McDowell, C., Werner, L., Bullock, H., and Fernald, J. (2002). *The Effects of Pair Programming in an Introductory Programming Course,* SIGCSE Conference Computer Science Education 2002.

Ruddick, S. (1989). *Maternal Thinking.* Boston: Beacon Press.

Williams, L. and Kessler, R. (2000). *The Effects of "Pair-Pressure" and "Pair-Learning" on Software Engineering Education,* Conference of Software Engineering Education and Training 2000.

Williams, L. and Kessler, R., (2000). "All I Really Need to Know about Pair Programming I Learned In Kindergarten," *Communications of the ACM,* May 2000.

Williams, L. and Kessler, R. (2001). "Experimenting with Industry's 'Pair-Programming' Model in the Computer Science Classroom," *Journal on Computer Science Education,* March 2001.

An Introduction to Test Driven Development

As stated in Chapter 23, many people have said they have really come to see the benefits of pair programming when they coupled pair programming and test driven development (TDD). Both pair programming and TDD have been practiced in isolation by programmers for many, many years. But the emergence of Extreme Programming has popularized both techniques. In Appendix D, we will briefly describe the TDD approach so that you can consider marrying the two together in your own development.

Examples

In order to demonstrate several points about TDD, two scenarios will be discussed.

Scenario One

Consider we want to write a function that adds two numbers. With TDD, the first thing we do is to write the first test case for this functionality. For example,

```
int sum = Calculator.sum(2,2);
assertEquals(4, sum);
```

In order to write this test case, some logical or interface design decisions were made: (1) There would be a calculator class; (2) the calculator class would have a sum method; and (3) the sum method would return an integer value.

Scenario Two

This simple example was based on one described by Kent Beck in IEEE Software (2001).

Suppose we want to write a function that, given a person of a certain age, returns the person's mortality table. We begin by writing

```
MortalityTable actualTable = new MortalityTable(bob);
AssertEquals(expectedTable, actualTable);
```

Now we need to create a Person "bob" to pass as a parameter to the MortalityTable constructor. To create a person, there is a Person constructor that takes 11 parameters. We start to add a line at the beginning of our test case to create "bob" so we can use the object to create an actualTable. We begin to write:

```
Person bob = new Person("Bob", "Newhart", 48, NON-SMOKER,
```

Then we realize that this constructor takes a lot of arguments—maybe there's a simpler way. Actually, to get a mortality table, all we really need to know is the age of the person and if he or she is a smoker. We do not have to create a Person at all. So we change our test case to

```
MortalityTable actualTable = new MortalityTable(48, NON-SMOKER);
```

After writing test cases that generally will not even compile, we create our physical design and implementation in order to pass these test cases. We incrementally think of every test case we can—to handle new functionality, to handle error conditions, and so on. We write a few test cases, implement the code, write a few test cases, implement the code, and so on. We keep our work within our intellectual control because we are continuually making small design and implementation decisions and increasing functionality at a relatively consistent rate.

Those who use the TDD approach profess the following benefits of the practice:

- TDD entices programmers to write code that is automatically testable, such as returning a value for Calculator.sum (in the first scenario) instead of having that method print the results to the screen. If programs are written without continual consideration toward being automatically testable, writing such test cases after the fact can be very difficult, if not impossible. Benefits of automated testing include: (1) production of a reliable system, (2) improvement of the quality of the test effort, and (3) reduction of the test effort and minimization of the schedule. (Dustin et al. 1999)

- Historically, "debugging is a bottleneck in programming (Ducasse and Emde 1988)." However, TDD provides the programmer with immediate feedback on the correctness of the code. As a result, defects and their causes can be easily identified. The defect must lie in the code that was just written or in code with which the recently added code interacts. An often cited tenet of software engineering, in concert with the Cost of Change (Boehm 1981), is that the longer a defect remains in a software system the more difficult and costly it is to remove. With TDD, defects are identified very quickly, and the source of the defect is more easily determined.

- The TDD test case assets create a through regression test bed. By continually running these automated test cases, one can easily identify if a change breaks anything in the existing system.

- The automated, extensive regression testing that is enabled by TDD should allow smooth integration of new functionality into the code base.

- As shown in the second scenario, TDD can make or alter our design decisions to simplify our code and add flexibility to our system

TDD is not meant to imply that test cases can be written only prior to code implementation. Additional test cases can certainly be added after code has been written. Specific integration tests are often written after code.

Some Results

Jeff Langr of ObjectMentor compares two implementations of identical code—one written without TDD and one with TDD. The original code had six methods (the average method size was 25 lines; the longest was over 100 lines of code) and 15 test cases. He found the code hard to modify. When he redid the code with TDD, the new code had 23 methods (average method size was five lines, the longest was 18 lines of code) and 20 tests. Small methods can increase maintainability, communicability, and extensibility of code (Langr 2001).

Additionally, Laurie and her graduate student, Boby George, ran a short, controlled TDD experiment with 150 students in her senior-level software engineering class at North Carolina State University (George 2002). The students were given a short programming problem to write code to compute bowling scores. The students were to implement the scoring during their 75-minute lab period (this was very time constrained). All students worked in pairs. Half the students were deemed TDD pairs while the other half were non-TDD pairs. The student code was tested using seven black box test cases. The results follow:

Number of Test Cases Passed	TDD	Non-TDD
0	9%	43%
1–3	41%	30%
4–7	50%	27%

Not only did the TDD pairs pass more test cases, but they also had programs with fewer lines of code. Programs that perform the same functionality with fewer lines of code are considered to have superior design and to require less maintenance costs (Boehm 1981).

TDD Without High-Low-Level Design

With Extreme Programming (XP), developers do not formally prepare high- or low-level designs. Developers work in pairs and informally apply any design techniques they feel are appropriate for the problem at hand. For example, they might brainstorm the class structure by performing a CRC card session (Bellin 1997) or draft out a UML class diagram (Fowler 2000; Jacobson et al. 1999) that is not inspected, archived, or shared. Alternatively, they start implementation by writing automated unit test cases without any design. For developers who work in this way, refactoring, as professed by Martin Fowler (1999), in concert with TDD is essential. Through refactoring, the internal structure of code is improved without altering its external behavior. With XP, developers understand that they might not arrive at the "best" design the first time they implement the code. After successfully writing test cases and implementing the code for new functionality, the developers look back through the code to see if any structural improvements can be made. The automated test cases give the developer the confidence that the structural improvements he or she makes do not alter the behavior of the system.

TDD With High-Low-Level Design

Many software development processes, particularly those involving life- and safety-critical applications, necessitate architectural, high- and low-level designs. TDD is just as beneficial to these processes. Consider Scenario One in this section of the proposal. If this software developer knew, based on his or her design documents, that there was a calculator class with a sum method, he or she would still write the test case before the code. With TDD after design, the developer is able to

- ensure the new functionality is automatically testable. Perhaps being automatically testable was not an initial design consideration; the developer can immediately alter the design to allow for testability.

- be provided with immediate feedback on the correctness of the new functionality. If the sum method is incorrect and the result of the sum method is incorporated into more complex functionality, problem determination is significantly more difficult once it is determined that the more complex functionality is not performing as expected.

- be provided with immediate feedback if the new functionality is causing undesirable behavior elsewhere in the code base; regression testing is automatically performed by running every test case that has been included in the code base. This feedback is predicated on the fact that the code base also has a thorough set of automated test cases.

- integrate his or her code into the code base without incident.

- alter the previously prepared design for simplicity or flexibility or new knowledge. Quite often, even meticulously prepared and inspected designs are changed when the code is actually implemented. This is not changed with TDD, although these changes might present themselves more rapidly through the short incremental development.

It is important to note that TDD can be implemented in essentially any development process simply by shifting from "unit test after implementing" to "unit test before implementing." Additionally, refactoring is a good practice in any process, although its criticality is lessened when architecture and design have been completed and inspected.

Tool Support

Many TDD programmers use the open source xUnit automated regression test frameworks. A complete listing of all supported languages, which includes Java, C++, http, Perl, Ruby, Scheme and Visual Basic is available at http://c2.com/cgi/wiki?TestingFramework. Other commercial tools are also available, including Silvermark Test Mentor and Parasoft JTest. The simplicity of the open source tools makes them the most popular among many TDD programmers.

References

Beck, K. (2001). "Aim, Fire," in *IEEE Software*, vol. 18, September/October 2001, pp. 87–89.

Bellin, D., and Simone, S. (1997). *The CRC Card Book*, Addison-Wesley.

Boehm, B. (1981). *Software Engineering Economics*, Prentice Hall.

Ducasse, M. and Emde, A. M. (1988). *A Review of Automated Debugging Systems: Knowledge, Strategies, and Techniques*, IEEE Computer Press.

Dustin, E., Rashka, J., and Paul, J. (1999). *Automated Software Testing*, Addison-Wesley.

Fowler, M. (2000). *UML Distilled, Second Edition: A Brief Guide to the Standard Object Modeling Language,* Addison-Wesley.

Fowler, M., Beck, K., Brant, J., Opdyke, W., and Roberts, D. (1999). *Refactoring: Improving the Design of Existing Code*, Addison-Wesley.

George, B. "Analysis and Quantification of the Test-Driven Development Approach," Master's Thesis, North Carolina State University.

Jacobson, I., Booch, G., and Rumbaugh, J., (1999). *The Unified Software Development Process*, Addison-Wesley.

Langr J., (2001). "Evolution of Test and Code Via Test-First Design," presented at OOPSLA 2001 http://www.objectmentor.com/resources/articles/tfd.pdf March 2001.

Index

Coverage, as a component of defect recovery efficiency, 228–229
Covey, Stephen, 206
Crashes, cause of, 39
CRC card sessions, 61, 175, 178, 185
    CSP and, 188
    TDD and, 248
Creativity, 60–61
CSP (Collaborative Software Process)
    case study, 181–191
    Focus Area 0 (baselining your process), 182–184, 186, 189
    Focus Area 1 (quality management), 182, 184–187
    Focus Area 2 (project management), 182, 187–190
Cubicles, arrangement of, 60, 69
Cultural issues, 56, 145–151
Cunningham, Ward, 14–15, 78, 172, 206
Customers
    cost of defects for, 39
    pairing of developers with, 196
    requirements definition and, 173–174

D

Database(s)
    experts, 59
    knowledge management and, 77
Debugging, 29, 70, 199, 247. *See also* Defects
Defect(s), 35, 40, 88. *See also* Code;
    Debugging; Quality
    CSP and, 186–187
    cost of, for customers, 39
    economic analysis and, 223, 228–229
    ego-less programming and, 204
    filters, 85–86
    multidisciplinary pairs and, 196
    pair debugging and, 29
    pair learning and, 30
    pair reviews and, 28–29
    recovery efficiency, 228–229
    quality assurance and, 85–86

DeMarco, Tom, 1, 15
    E-Factor in, 24–25
    flow state in, 19, 20
Dependency problems, 58
Desks, arrangement of, 60
Disagreements, resolving, 61, 90–92, 207–208
Disbelief, suspending, 56
Discounting, 227
Discount rate, 227
Distributed
    cognition, 26
    pair programming, 60, 197–199
"Do Food" strategy, 49, 54
Drink vending machine program, 74
Driver(s). *See also* Pairs
    asking questions and, 92
    conflict resolution and, 90
    ego problems and, 159–167
    expert-average pairs and, 106
    multidisciplinary pairs and, 196
    professional, problem of, 153–156
    projection screens and, 196–197
    role of, rotating, 63
    tips for working with, 89
    use of the term, 4
    workplace layout and, 67, 69
    XP and, 178
Dual video cards, 68–69

E

Early Adopters, 54, 55
Early Majority, use of the term, 48
Earned value. *See* EV (Earned Value)
Economic analysis, 221–236
    economic comparison model for, 226–232
    introduction to, 221–223
Edge Learning Institute, 35
Education. *See also* Teaching; Training;
    Tutorials
    benefits of pair programming to, 237–243
    issues to consider, 240–241

F

Franklin, Aretha, 98
Functional testing, 87, 185

G

Gabriel, Dick, 8, 12–13
"Gang of Four," 213
Gartner Group, 39
Gender issues, 139–143
George, Boby, 248
Germany, 148, 149, 198
Gibson, Richard G., 13
Glass, Robert, 60–61
Goals
    changing behavior to reach, 35–36
    pair negotiation and, 26
    WIFM thoughts and, 35–36
Gold Collar Worker (Kelley), 25
"Go/no-go" decisions, 188
Green, Gina, 51–53
Griss, Martin, 9, 100–101
Group(s)
    size of, 84–85
    testing, 86
GUI (graphical user interface) programming,
    59, 74–75, 102

H

Handicapped individuals, 154, 155
Hartman, Bob, 88
Harvard University, 39, 53
Hayes, Steve, 95, 102, 120–121, 142
Herman, Eric, 125, 162
Hevner, Alan, 51–53
Hewlett-Packard, 100, 223
Hill Air Force Base, 36–37
Hometown Stories, use of the term, 49, 54
Houston, Greg, 109, 114
HTML (HyperText Markup Language),
    237–238
Humility, practicing, 203–204
Humphrey, Watts S., 85, 181–182, 190, 224
Hutchins, E. L., 26

I

IBM (International Business Machines), 35,
    83, 223
IEEE Software (journal), 60–61, 246
Incremental realized value. *See* IRV
    (Incrementally Realized Value)
Increments, defined, 172
India, 40, 41, 149, 198
India Technology, 40, 41
Innovation
    adoption rates, 47
    transitioning to pair programming and,
        46–49, 52–57
Innovators, use of the term, 46–49, 54
Integration issues, 69
Intent, use of the term, 94
Intercommunication costs, 44
Interruptions, avoiding, 19–20, 24–25
Introducing Patterns into Organizations
    (Manns and Rising), 46–47
Introvert(s)
    excess ego problems and, 160
    importance of communication skills to,
        205–206
    -introvert pairs, 133–138
"Involve Everyone" strategy, 55
IRV (Incrementally Realized Value), 229,
    232–233

J

Jacobson, Ivar, 9
Jangr, Jeff, 248
Japan, 148
Java, 250
JavaScript, 238
Jeffries, Ron, 98, 115, 120, 125, 172
    on ego problems, 166
    on gender issues, 142
    on the professional driver problem, 156
Jones, C., 223, 228
Jonker, Todd, 136, 166

Jonsson, Patrick, 9
JTest (Parasoft), 250
"Just Do It" principle, 47, 54

K

Kernel, 59
Keyboards
    professional driver problem and, 153–156
    using two, 68–69
    wireless, 68
    workplace layout and, 67–69
Kleb, Bil, 41, 69, 91
Knowledge. *See also* Education; Learning;
    Training
    expert-expert pairing and, 102
    management strategies, 17, 77–79
    pair learning and, 30–31
    pair rotation and, 73–82
    pair understanding exercises and, 212–214
    social construction of, 25–26
    synergy and, 25–26
    transfer, improved, through pair
        programming, 5, 30–31, 73–82
Kohnke, Jennifer, 94
Kotter, John, 53

L

Labor cost, 226
Lance, Mike, 120, 135–136
Langr, Jeff, 126, 136
Language(s)
    foreign, 148–149
    pattern, 8, 9, 46–49, 53–54
Laptop computers, 69
Latency, 228–229
Lave, J., 30
LCDs (liquid crystal displays), 8. *See also*
    Monitors
Leaders, local, use of the term, 48, 53–54. *See
    also* Coaches; Managers
Learning. *See also* Education; Knowledge;
    Training

enhanced, through pair programming, 5,
    237–243
expert-expert pairing and, 102
listening and, 207
through mentoring, 36, 74, 80–81, 92,
    106–109, 112–116
pair, 30–31, 119–121, 199–200
pair rotation and, 77–81
paradigms, 199
Lichtenwalner, Lee, 149
Life-cycle evolution, 171–172, 182
Lindner, Michael, 102, 108–109, 142, 157
Lisp, 8, 12, 13, 100–101
Listening. *See also* Communication
    active, 91
    introverts and, 134–135
    overall importance of, 206–207
Lister, T., 15, 19, 20, 24–25
Local Leaders, use of the term, 48, 53–54
Lowe, Iain, 167
Lucid, 12

M

McBreen, Pete, 205–206
McCarthy, Jim, 56, 165–166
McCarthy, Michele, 56
MacCormack, Alan, 39
Mackinnon, Tim, 157
MacLisp, 12
Malik, William, 39
Management. *See also* Managers
    knowledge, 17, 77–79
    organizational patterns and, 46–47, 76,
        212–214
    project, 187–190
    quality, 184–187
    time, strategies for, 25
    by Walking Around (MBWA), 63, 160–161,
        240–241
Managers. *See also* Management
    advice for, 53–56
    conflict resolution and, 90

Nonverbal behavior, 26
North Carolina State University, 197, 199–200, 248
Northeastern University, 3
Nosek, J. T., 37
Novice(s)
    asking for help and, 28
    characterization of, 95
    -expert pairs, 16–17, 62–63, 80–81, 111–116, 120–121
    -novice pairs, 117–121, 238
    pair learning and, 30–31
NPV (Net Present Value), 222, 229–234
Nynex, 77–78

O

Objectives
    of management, 34–45
    of pair programming tutorials, 212
Organizational
    guidelines, 55
    patterns, 46–47, 76, 212–214
Organizational Patterns (Coplien), 212
Overconfidence, 61–62. *See also* Confidence

P

Pair(s). *See also* Pair programming
    brainstorming, 27
    courage, 27–28
    cultural issues and, 145–151
    debugging, 10, 29
    developer-customer, 196
    ego problems and, 159–162
    expert-average, 105–109
    expert-expert, 17, 97–103
    expert-novice, 16–17, 62–63, 80–81, 111–116, 120–121
    extrovert-extrovert, 123–127
    extrovert-introvert, 128–133
    flow state and, 19–20
    introvert-introvert, 133–138
    learning, 30–31, 119–121, 199–200

multidisciplinary, 195–196
    negotiation, 25–27, 89–90
    novice-novice, 117–121, 238
    pressure, 22–25, 38, 53, 62
    problems faced by, 16–17, 58–64
    reviews, 28–29
    selecting, principles for, 93–96
    seven habits of effective, 203–209
    synergistic behavior of, 22–33
    tips and tricks for, 89–92
Pair programming. *See also* Pairs
    advantages/disadvantages of, 4–5
    casual use of, 34, 63
    defined, 4
    as enjoyable, 22
    Gabriel's historical account of, 12–13
    as an integral part of XP, 177–178
    intensity of, 16
    introduction to, 1, 3–13
    life-cycle affordability of, 40–41
    mandated, 50–56
    presentations, 50–51, 215–217
    readiness surveys, 50
    seven myths of, 14–21
    seven synergistic behaviors of, 22–33
    timelines, 8–9
    tips and tricks, 89–92
    transitioning to, by choice, 50–57
    two levels of, 34
Pair rotation
    advantages of, 73
    assignment of, 75–76
    Beck on, 30–31
    daily meetings and, 76
    examples of, 5–8, 217–219
    group size and, 84–85
    intercommunication costs and, 44
    knowledge management and, 77–79
    logistics and, 75–76
    overview of, 73–82
    pair learning and, 30–31
    survey data on, 16–17

training and, 79–81
Parasoft JTest, 250
Parkinson's Law, 22, 86
Pasteur project, 9
Patterns
    language, 8, 9, 46–49, 53–54
    organizational, 46–47, 76, 212–214
    pair understanding and, 212–214
Paulk, Mark, 181
pcAnywhere, 198
Peer(s)
    acceptance strategies, 46–49
    evaluations/reviews, 18, 83–84, 181
    gaining the support of, 46–49
Peeters, Vera, 125, 141
Pekeler, Christian, 148
Pentagon, 223
Peopleware (DeMarco and Lister), 15, 19–20, 24–25
Performance appraisals, 83–84. *See also* Reviews
Personality types, 61–63, 71. *See also* Egos; Extroverts; Introverts
    Meyers-Briggs test for, 134
    performance appraisals and, 83–84
    skill imbalances and, 62
Personal Software Process. *See* PSP (Personal Software Process)
Personal Touch, use of the term, 47, 54
Pfister, Markus, 158
Pieces of Clay, use of the term, 49
Pilots, 35, 55
Portland Pattern Repository (Cunningham), 14–15
Power, desire for, 154
PowerPoint (Microsoft), 215–216
Presentations, 50–51, 215–216. *See also* Tutorials
Present Value. *See* PV (Present Value)
Pressure, increased, 22–25, 38, 53, 62
Privacy policy, 6
Procedures. *See* Standards

Processes, baselining, 182–184. *See also* PSP (Personal Software Process)
Productivity measures, 36–37, 224, 224, 225. *See also* Reviews
Programming, use of the term, 10
Projection screens, 196–197, 198–199. *See also* Monitors
PSP (Personal Software Process), 181–190
    earned value in, 189–190
    quality metrics and, 187
    test cases and, 186
    time-tracking procedures, 183
Psychology, 26, 203–204. *See also* Personality types
Psychology of Computer Programming, The (Weinberg), 203–204
PV (Present Value), 226–227

Q

Quality. *See also* Defects
    assurance (QA), 85–86, 88
    CSP and, 184–187
    improved, through pair programming, 4
    of Service parameters, 41
Questions, asking, 28, 92, 107

R

Raytheon, 223
"Read my Lips: No New Process Models" (Weigers), 182
Recognition, sharing, 17–18, 56
Refactoring, 94, 155, 161–162, 165–166, 250
Reflective articulation, 78, 206. *See also* Communication
Regression testing, 247, 249–250
Rekitt, Norman, 120, 162
Release
    defined, 172
    planning, 172–173
Religion, 102
repetitive strain injuries (RSIs), 98, 100, 154

Requirements
    CSP and, 185, 186
    definition, 173–174
Resistance, to paired programming, 14–21,
        34–45
    inviting, as a strategy, 54–55
    by management, 14–21, 34–45
    misconceptions and, 14–21
    pair rotation and, 75–76
    transitioning to pair programming and,
        50–56
Respect, importance of, 98–99
Respected Techie, use of the term, 49, 54
Reviews
    continuous, 18–19, 30
    design, 85–86
    formal code, 35
    pair learning and, 30
    peer, 18, 83–84, 181
    quality assurance and, 85–86
Rework
    effort, 224–225
    time, 183
Rice University, 3
Rising, Linda, 46, 53
Risk(s)
    assessments, 172
    of losing key team members, reducing,
        41–42
    -mitigation strategies, 46
Rogers, Jason, 47, 49, 125–126, 149
Root causes, use of the term, 94
Royce, Winton, 171–172
RSIs (repetitive strain injuries), 98, 100, 154

S

Scalability, 41
Schedules, 16, 36–41
    coordinating, between pairs, 22
    flex hours and, 60
    pair rotation and, 74
    problems with, 58–59, 60

Schwaber, K., 10
SCRUM
    books on, 10
    economic analysis and, 228
    meetings, 5, 76
    pair rotation and, 76
SEI (Software Engineering Institute), 181,
        182, 223
Self-esteem, 165. *See also* Confidence
Shopping carts, 6
Shukla, Anuja, 80
Siemens, 198
Silvermark Test Mentor, 250
Sisk, John, 167
Skepticism, being prepared for, 54–55
Sociology, 206
Socratic dialogues, 92
Software Development with SCRUM (Beedle
    and Schwaber), 10
Software Factory model, 227–232, 234
Software Reuse (Griss, Jacobson, and
    Johnson), 9
Solo programmers, 15–16, 19–20, 28
    creativity and, 60–61
    economic analysis and, 222–226
    experience of mental flow by, 19
    Glass on, 60–61
    impact of noise on, 71
    problems encountered by, after
        getting used to pair programming,
        58
    references to, as mavericks, 93
Spiral development model, 172
Standards, 25, 91, 177
Stand-up meetings, 5
Stanford University, 12
Steele, Guy L., Jr., 13
Stereotypes, 205–206
Stotts, David, 197, 198
Strategic
    defects, defined, 4
    programmers, 102

WIIFM (What's In It For Me) thoughts, 35–36, 42–43
Win-win negotiating tactics, 188
Windows XP (Microsoft), 83
Wood, Bill, 41, 69, 91
Work
    "expands to fill the time available" (Parkinson's Law"), 22, 86
    -load, increased, concerns about, 39–40
    unit, 222
Workplace layout
    arrangement of cubicles, 60, 69
    arrangement of desks, 60
    overview of, 67–71
positioning of chairs, 67
    positioning of keyboards, 67–69
    use of projection screens in, 196–197, 198–199
Wright, Bill, 8
Writing Effective Use Cases (Cockburn), 185

X

XP (eXtreme Programming)
    acceptance testing and, 177, 186
    books on, 10, 14, 16, 58, 70
    case study, 171–179
    code implementation, 176–177

coding standards, 177
commenting guidelines, 177
continuous integration and, 177
CRC cards and, 185
CSP and, 181, 183, 189–190
design philosophy, 175–176
development of, 9, 172–173
distributed pair programming and, 198
economic analysis and, 228
meetings, 76
pair programming as an integral part of, 177–178
pair rotation and, 76
quality metrics and, 187
release planning, 172–173
requirements definition, 173–174
testing and, 87, 91, 176–178, 186, 245, 248–249
working alone and, 15
XP Applied (Auer and Miller), 70
xUnit, 250

Y

YAGNI (You Aren't Gonna Need It) philosophy, 175–177

Also Available from Addison-Wesley

0-201-77639-1

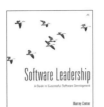

0-201-70044-1

0-201-71516-3

0-201-73721-3

0-201-77577-8

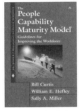

0-201-60445-0

0-201-78606-0

0-201-73500-8

0-201-61626-2

0-201-60444-2

0-201-54809-7

0-201-54597-7

0-201-54610-8

0-201-54664-7

0-201-18095-2

From the XP Series

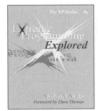

0-201-73397-8

0-201-61640-8

0-201-71091-9

0-201-70937-6

0-201-71040-4

0-201-70842-6

0-201-61641-6